HSK 1

STORYBOOK

Vol. 3

Stories in Simplified Chinese and Pinyin

150 Words Vocabulary Level

B.Y. LEONG

ISBN: 9781077665477

Edited by Y.L Hoe

Book Cover by Sok Yeng Leong

Publisher:

Leong Bik Yoke

C1013 Centum@Oasis Corporate Park,
No.2, Jalan PJU1A/2, Ara Damansara
47301 Petaling Jaya, Selangor
MALAYSIA

feedback@allmusing.net

Table of Contents

INTRODUCTION

HSK 1 Storybook Vol. 3 consists of 10 short stories written in Simplified Chinese and Pinyin. The purpose of this book is to provide readers with reading materials to practice their reading skills as well as an introduction to more extended sentence structure and longer articles. The stories here are of course different compared to the stories in the first book.

HSK 1 Storybook Vol. 3 has all the vocabularies in HSK 1. If you finish the book, you would have practiced your reading skill on all the vocabularies in HSK 1.

I have tried to restrict the vocabularies used in this book to HSK 1 as far as possible. Where it is not possible, I have introduced limited new words in the story. If you have learned all the HSK 1 Vocabulary and completed the Standard Course Book for HSK 1 by Jiang Liping, you would be able to read about 85% of this book (and if you have learnt the new words in HSK 1 Storybook Vol. 2, you would be able to read more than 95% of this book) without learning new words.

I consider the HSK 1 Vocabulary together with the new words introduced in Standard Course Book as *Extended HSK 1 Vocabulary* and I will refer to it as such from now on.

The structure of this book is as follows:

- **Statistics** – this will provide the reader with an analysis of the words used in the story and the level of difficulty. It will set out new words along with Pinyin and explanation. The new words set out here are not cumulative. New words are set out here as long as the words used are not in the Extended HSK 1 Vocabulary.

- **Story** – this section is the story in Simplified Chinese without Pinyin and the English translation. To test level of reading skills, you should attempt to read this section first before going to the next.
- **Pinyin and Translation** – this will be the section for Pinyin and English translation.
- **Appendix** – for the benefit of those who need assistance on the HSK 1 and HSK 1 Standard Course vocabularies, I have included them in this section for your reference.

The stories in this book are individual stories. A reader may choose to read this book in any particular order. To help you decide which story to read first, you may take a look at the statistics before you begin. The difficulty level for each story varies.

Text to speech for this book has been enabled. You may also download the **free audio files** with the link and password provided on the last page.

Presumably, you would have read the first 2 volumes before embarking on this book. If you have enjoyed reading all the books, please leave a review or comment to let us know what do you think.

Happy reading!

B.Y Leong

HSK Storybook Series:-

HSK 1 Storybook

HSK 1 Storybook Vol. 2

HSK 1 Storybook Vol. 3

HSK 2 Storybook Vol. 1

HSK 2 Storybook Vol. 2

HSK 2 Storybook Vol. 3

HSK 3 Storybook, HSK 4 Storybook and other titles coming soon.

Go to https://allmusing.net to download sample chapters and free audio files.

Statistics for Story [1]

644 Total Word Count

126 Number of Unique Words

85 (56.67 %) of the 150 HSK 1 words are used in this Story

83.39 % of the Story comprise of the Extended HSK 1 words

22 New Words

New Words	Pinyin	Explanation
它	tā	It
走	zǒu	To walk, to go
小五	Xiǎo Wǔ	Name of a person
到	dào	Arrive, up to (verb complement denoting completion or result of an action)
已经	yǐjīng	Already, have
只	zhǐ	Only, merely, just, classifier for dogs, cats, birds and certain animals
见	jiàn	See, meet

New Words	Pinyin	Explanation
如果	rú guǒ	If, in case, in the event that
可是	kěshì	But, however
再	zài	Again
小亮	Xiǎo Liàng	Name of a person
过	guò	Over, cross, pass (time)
就	jiù	At once, right away, as soon as, then, in that case
快	kuài	Fast, quickly, soon
天天	tiān tiān	Everyday
别	bié	Other, another, don’t
先	xiān	Prior, first, in advance
为什么	wèishéme	Why
还	hái	Also, still, yet
让	ràng	Let, allow
出	chū	Out
养	yǎng	To raise or keep animals or pets

[1] Our Dog is Missing

我们的狗不见了

我有一只狗，它的名字是小五。它今年八岁了。爸爸，妈妈和我都很爱它。它天天都很喜欢走来走去。有时候它会走到前面的商店，有时候它会走到后面的饭馆。可是小五已经好几天没回家了。我们去商店没看见它，去饭馆也没看见它。我工作时，爸爸妈妈就去问，有没有人看到小五。

爸爸：先生，你看见我的狗吗？它是这样的。

先生：你的狗很漂亮啊。对不起，我没看见。

爸爸：谢谢。小姐，你看见我的狗吗？它是这样的。

小姐：对不起，我没看见。

妈妈：好了。你先坐一下吧。天气很热。我们坐一下再走，好吗？

爸爸：不好。小五已经好几天没回家了。如果我问多点儿人我们能快点儿看到小五的。你想不想再看到小五呢？

妈妈：我很想看到它。可是，你不能这样的走来走去。能不能坐在这儿十分钟？你上午走到下午，也没吃饭，你不能这样的。十分钟后，我和你一起问人有没有看到小五，好不好？

爸爸：好吧。我们只在这儿坐十分钟。十分钟后，你和我一起走。

十分钟后：

爸爸：我们现在走吧。

妈妈：你认识那个人吗？

爸爸：哪个人啊？

妈妈：在那个小姐的前面。看见吗？

爸爸：看见了。是谁啊？我不认识他。你认识他吗？

妈妈：我不认识他。可是你看，在他后面的那只狗，是不是小五啊？

爸爸：我们快点儿过去看看吧。

爸爸妈妈前看，后看，在看那只狗是不是小五。

爸爸：你看怎么样？

妈妈：我们过去问一问那个先生，他什么时候有这只狗。

爸爸：先生，你好。

先生：你好。今天天气很好。很多天都没看见这样的天气了。你们也出来走走吗？

爸爸：我们家的狗不见了。它已经好几天没回家了。它很喜欢走来走去。我们走到这儿都还没看见它。

先生：你们的狗是怎么样的？

爸爸：是这样的。

先生：如果我看见你的狗，我会打个电话给你的。再见。

爸爸：先生，你的狗是哪儿来的？

先生：是我儿子几年前买给我的。为什么？

妈妈：没什么。它让我们想到小五。

先生：它不是你们的小五啊！它是我的小亮。小亮今年六岁了。我已经养了它六年了。

爸爸：对不起。我们是太想小五了。

先生：没关系。我天天都会和小亮来这儿走走。如果我看见你们的狗，我会打个电话给你们的。

妈妈：太谢谢你了。

先生：不客气。再见。

爸爸：那不是小五。

妈妈：不是小五。你坐在这儿，我去买点儿水给你喝。

爸爸：也买点儿水果吧。小五很爱吃水果的。

妈妈：我买些苹果吧。你坐在这儿，别走来走去。

喝了水，吃了苹果后，妈妈就叫爸爸回家，明天再来这儿。爸爸妈妈回到家里的时候，小五已经回到家里了。爸爸妈妈很高兴看见它。

Pinyin and Translation [1]

我有一只狗，它的名字是小五。它今年八岁了。爸爸，妈妈和我都很爱它。它天天都很喜欢走来走去。有时候它会走到前面的商店，有时候它会走到后面的饭馆。可是小五已经好几天没回家了。我们去商店没看见它，去饭馆也没看见它。我工作时，爸爸妈妈就去问，有没有人看到小五。

Wǒ yǒuyī zhǐ gǒu, tā de míngzì shì Xiǎo Wǔ. Tā jīnnián bā suìle. Bàba, māmā hé wǒ dōu hěn ài tā. Tā tiāntiān dōu hěn xǐhuān zǒu lái zǒu qù. Yǒu shíhòu tā huì zǒu dào qiánmiàn de shāngdiàn, yǒu shíhòu tā huì zǒu dào hòumiàn de fànguǎn. Kěshì Xiǎo Wǔ yǐjīng hǎo jǐ tiān méi huí jiāle. Wǒmen qù shāngdiàn méi kànjiàn tā, qù fànguǎn yě méi kànjiàn tā. Wǒ gōngzuò shí, bàba māmā jiù qù wèn, yǒu méiyǒu rén kàn dào Xiǎo Wǔ.

I have a dog whose name is Xiao Wu. It is eight years old this year. Dad, Mom and I love it very much. It likes to walk around every day. Sometimes it will go to the store in front, sometimes it will go to the restaurant behind. However, Xiao Wu has not returned home for several days. We didn't see it when we went to the store, and we didn't see it at the restaurant. When I went to work, Mom and Dad went around asking if anyone saw Xiao Wu.

爸爸：先生，你看见我的狗吗？它是这样的。

Bàba: Xiānshēng, nǐ kànjiàn wǒ de gǒu ma? Tā shì zhèyàng de.

Dad: Sir, have you seen my dog? It looks like this.

先生：你的狗很漂亮啊。对不起，我没看见。

Xiānshēng: Nǐ de gǒu hěn piàoliang a. Duìbùqǐ, wǒ méi kànjiàn.

Sir: Your dog is very beautiful. Sorry, I didn't see it.

爸爸：谢谢。小姐，你看见我的狗吗？它是这样的。

Bàba: Xièxiè. Xiǎojiě, nǐ kànjiàn wǒ de gǒu ma? Tā shì zhèyàng de.

Dad: Thank you. Miss, have you seen my dog? It looks like this.

小姐：对不起，我没看见。

Xiǎo jiě: Duìbùqǐ, wǒ méi kànjiàn.

Miss: Sorry, I didn't see it.

妈妈：好了。你先坐一下吧。天气很热。我们坐一下再走，好吗？

Māmā: Hǎole. Nǐ xiān zuò yīxià ba. Tiānqì hěn rè. Wǒmen zuò yīxià zài zǒu, hǎo ma?

Mom: Ok. Let's sit down first. The weather is hot. Let's sit down for a while, ok?

爸爸：不好。小五已经好几天没回家了。如果我问多点儿人我们能快点儿看到小五的。你想不想再看到小五呢？

Bàba: Bù hǎo. Xiǎo Wǔ yǐjīng hǎo jǐ tiān méi huí jiāle. Rúguǒ wǒ wèn duō diǎn er rén wǒmen néng kuài diǎn er kàn dào Xiǎo Wǔ de. Nǐ xiǎng bùxiǎng zài kàn dào Xiǎo Wǔ ne?

Dad: No. Xiao Wu has not returned home for several days. If I ask more people, we can see Xiao Wu sooner. Don't you want to see Xiao Wu again?

妈妈：我很想看到它。可是，你不能这样的走来走去。能不能坐在这儿十分钟？你上午走到下午，也没吃饭，你不能这样的。十分钟后，我和你一起问人有没有看到小五，好不好？

Māmā: Wǒ hěn xiǎng kàn dào tā. Kěshì, nǐ bùnéng zhèyàng de zǒu lái zǒu qù. Néng bùnéng zuò zài zhè'er shí fēnzhōng?

Nǐ shàngwǔ zǒu dào xiàwǔ, yě méi chīfàn, nǐ bùnéng zhèyàng de. Shí fēnzhōng hòu, wǒ hé nǐ yīqǐ wèn rén yǒu méiyǒu kàn dào xiǎo wǔ, hǎobù hǎo?

Mom: Of course I want to see it. However, you can't walk around like this. Can you sit here for ten minutes? You went from morning to afternoon and you didn't eat. You can't do this. 10 minutes later, I will go with you to ask around if anyone saw Xiao Wu, okay?

爸爸：好吧。我们只在这儿坐十分钟。十分钟后，你和我一起走。

Bàba: Hǎo ba. Wǒmen zhǐ zài zhè'er zuò shí fēnzhōng. Shí fēnzhōng hòu, nǐ hé wǒ yīqǐ zǒu.

Dad: Ok. We only sit here for 10 minutes. After 10 minutes, you will go with me.

十分钟后：

Shí fēnzhōng hòu:

10 minutes later:

爸爸：我们现在走吧。

Bàba: Wǒmen xiànzài zǒu ba.

Dad: Let's go now.

妈妈：你认识那个人吗？

Māmā: Nǐ rènshì nàgè rén ma?

Mom: Do you know that person?

爸爸：哪个人啊？

Bàba: Nǎge rén a?

Dad: Which person?

妈妈：在那个小姐的前面。看见吗？

Māmā: Zài nàgè xiǎojiě de qiánmiàn. Kànjiàn ma?

Mom: In front of the lady. Do you see him?

爸爸：看见了。是谁啊？我不认识他。你认识他吗？

Bàba: Kànjiànle. Shì shéi a? Wǒ bù rènshì tā. Nǐ rènshì tā ma?

Dad: I see him. Who is that? I do not know him. Do you know him?

妈妈：我不认识他。可是你看，在他后面的那只狗，是不是小五啊？

Māmā: Wǒ bù rènshì tā. Kěshì nǐ kàn, zài tā hòumiàn dì nà zhǐ gǒu, shì bùshì xiǎo wǔ a?

Mom: I don't know him. But do you see, the dog behind him, is it Xiao Wu?

爸爸：我们快点儿过去看看吧。

Bàba: Wǒmen kuài diǎn er guòqù kàn kàn ba.

Dad: Let's go over and have a look.

爸爸妈妈前看，后看，在看那只狗是不是小五。

Bàba māmā qián kàn, hòu kàn, zài kàn nà zhǐ gǒu shì bùshì Xiǎo Wǔ.

Mom and Dad look at it, again and again, to see if the dog was Xiao Wu.

爸爸：你看怎么样？

Bàba: Nǐ kàn zěnme yàng?

Dad: What do you think?

妈妈：我们过去问一问那个先生，他什么时候有这只狗。

Māmā: Wǒmen guòqù wèn yī wèn nàgè xiānshēng, tā shénme shíhòu yǒu zhè zhǐ gǒu.

Mom: We go over and ask the gentleman since when did he have this dog.

爸爸：先生，你好。

Bàba: Xiānshēng, nǐ hǎo.

Dad: How are you, Sir?

先生：你好。今天天气很好。很多天都没看见这样的天气了。你们也出来走走吗？

Xiānshēng: Nǐ hǎo. Jīntiān tiānqì hěn hǎo. Hěnduō tiān dōu méi kànjiàn zhèyàng de tiānqìle. Nǐmen yě chūlái zǒu zǒu ma?

Sir: Hello. The weather is very good today. I haven't seen such good weather for many days. Are you guys going out for a walk, too?

爸爸：我们家的狗不见了。它已经好几天没回家了。它很喜欢走来走去。我们走到这儿都还没看见它。

Bàba: Wǒmen jiā de gǒu bùjiànle. Tā yǐjīng hǎo jǐ tiān méi huí jiāle. Tā hěn xǐhuān zǒu lái zǒu qù. Wǒmen zǒu dào zhè'er dōu hái méi kànjiàn tā.

Dad: Our family dog is missing. It hasn't been home for days. It likes to run around. We haven't seen it here.

先生：你们的狗是怎么样的？

Xiānshēng: Nǐmen de gǒu shì zěnme yàng de?

Sir: What is your dog like?

爸爸：是这样的。

Bàba: Shì zhèyàng de.

Dad: It looks like this.

先生：如果我看见你的狗，我会打个电话给你的。再见。

Xiānshēng: Rúguǒ wǒ kànjiàn nǐ de gǒu, wǒ huì dǎ gè diànhuà gěi nǐ de. Zàijiàn.

Sir: If I see your dog, I will call you. Goodbye.

爸爸：先生，你的狗是哪儿来的？

Bàba: Xiānshēng, nǐ de gǒu shì nǎ'er lái de?

Dad: Where did your dog come from, Sir?

先生：是我儿子几年前买给我的。为什么？

Xiānshēng: Shì wǒ érzi jǐ nián qián mǎi gěi wǒ de. Wèishéme?

Sir: My son bought it for me a few years ago. Why?

妈妈：没什么。它让我们想到小五。

Māmā: Méishénme. Tā ràng wǒmen xiǎngdào Xiǎo Wǔ.

Mom: Nothing. It makes us think of Xiao Wu.

先生：它不是你们的小五啊！它是我的小亮。小亮今年六岁了。我已经养了它六年了。

Xiānshēng: Tā bùshì nǐmen de Xiǎo Wǔ a! Tā shì wǒ de Xiǎo Liàng. Xiǎo Liàng jīnnián liù suìle. Wǒ yǐjīng yǎngle tā liù niánle.

Sir: It's not your Xiao Wu! It's my Xiao Liang. Xiao Liang is six years old this year. I've been raising it for six years.

爸爸：对不起。我们是太想小五了。

Bàba: Duìbùqǐ. Wǒmen shì tài xiǎng xiǎo wǔle.

Dad: I'm sorry. We miss Xiao Wu too much.

先生：没关系。我天天都会和小亮来这儿走走。如果我看见你们的狗，我会打个电话给你们的。

Xiānshēng: Méiguānxì. Wǒ tiāntiān dūhuì hé Xiǎo Liàng lái zhè'er zǒu zǒu. Rúguǒ wǒ kànjiàn nǐmen de gǒu, wǒ huì dǎ gè diànhuà gěi nǐmen de.

Sir: Never mind. I go for walks with Xiao Liang every day. If I see your dog, I'll give you a call.

妈妈：太谢谢你了。

Māmā: Tài xièxiè nǐle.

Mom: Thank you so much.

先生：不客气。再见。

Xiānshēng: Bù kèqì. Zàijiàn.

Sir: You're welcome. Good bye.

爸爸：那不是小五。

Bàba: Nà bùshì Xiǎo Wǔ.

Dad: That's not a Xiao Wu.

妈妈：不是小五。你坐在这儿，我去买点儿水给你喝。

Māmā: Bùshì Xiǎo Wǔ. Nǐ zuò zài zhè'er, wǒ qù mǎidiǎn er shuǐ gěi nǐ hē.

Mom: It's not Xiao Wu. You sit here, I'll go and buy you some water to drink.

爸爸：也买点儿水果吧。小五很爱吃水果的。

Bàba: Yě mǎidiǎn er shuǐguǒ ba. Xiǎo Wǔ hěn ài chī shuǐguǒ de.

Dad: Buy some fruits, too. Xiao Wu likes to eat fruits very much.

妈妈：我买些苹果吧。你坐在这儿，别走来走去。

Māmā: Wǒ mǎi xiē píngguǒ ba. Nǐ zuò zài zhè'er, bié zǒu lái zǒu qù.

Mom: Let me buy some apples. You sit here and don't walk around.

喝了水，吃了苹果后，妈妈就叫爸爸回家，明天再来这儿。爸爸妈妈回到家里的时候，小五已经回到家里了。爸爸妈妈很高兴看见它。

Hēle shuǐ, chīle píngguǒ hòu, māmā jiù jiào bàba huí jiā, míngtiān zàilái zhè'er. Bàba māmā huí dào jiālǐ de shíhòu, xiǎo wǔ yǐjīng huí dào jiālǐle. Bàba māmā hěn gāoxìng kànjiàn tā.

After drinking some water and eating some apples, Mom asked Dad to go home and come back again tomorrow. When Mom and Dad returned home, Xiao Wu had already returned home. Mom and Dad were very happy to see it.

Statistics for Story [2]

621 Total Word Count

106 Number of Unique Words

67 (44.67 %) of the 150 HSK 1 words are used in this Story

88.89 % of the Story comprise of the Extended HSK 1 words

22 New Words

New Words	Pinyin	Explanation
用	yòng	Use
就	jiù	At once, right away, as soon as, then, in that case
因为	yīnwèi	Because, since, for
快	kuài	Fast, quickly, soon
到	dào	Arrive, up to (verb complement denoting completion or result of an action)
为什么	wèishéme	Why
如果	rú guǒ	If, in case, in the event that
过	guò	Over, cross, pass (time)

New Words	Pinyin	Explanation
让	ràng	Let, allow
卖	mài	Sell, sale
先	xiān	Prior, first, in advance
但是	dàn shì	But, however
才	cái	only
比	bǐ	Compare, contrast
只	zhǐ	Only, merely, just, classifier for dogs, cats, birds and certain animals
已经	yǐjīng	Already, have
难	nán	Difficult
听说	tīng shuō	Heard
可是	kěshì	But, however
别	bié	Other, another
出	chū	Out
还	hái	Also, still, yet

[2] Studying with a Computer

用电脑学习

在学校里有很多人会用电脑。我和同学们都会用电脑。可是家里的爸爸妈妈就不会用电脑。老师让我问爸爸妈妈能不能买个电脑在家里用。昨天爸爸出去的时候在下雨，他回到家的时候很不高兴，我就没问他能不能买电脑了。

今天他看来是高兴一点儿。这是因为他的汉语老师说他写的字很好。他回到家的时候就叫我们一起去饭馆吃饭了。

在饭馆里：

我：爸爸，老师让我问你能不能买个电脑在家里用。因为学校里的电脑很少，太多同学们用电脑了。如果家里有个电脑，我就能在家里学习和写字了。

爸爸：为什么用电脑学习和写字呢？你不是用书吗？

我：用电脑来写字会写的快点儿，学习也会学的快点儿。

爸爸：是吗？我在学习汉语时也没用电脑。我的老师也没叫我买电脑。我不是买了很多书给你吗？

我：是啊爸爸，你买了很多书给我，但是只用书是不能的。学校里，同学们都用电脑，我的老师也用电脑。我怎么能不用电脑呢？

爸爸：我看你的学校和老师是多做的。

我：不是啊。很多同学的家里已经有电脑了。如果我们不买电脑，就会很难学习，因为别的同学会比我学的快。

爸爸：我用书来学习，没用电脑，我不还是学的很快吗。你为什么不能？

我：爸爸，我怎么样说你才会买电脑给我呢？

爸爸：买电脑用很多钱的。你就用书来学习吧。

我：我有一个同学，他买电脑不是用了很多钱。他说有一个商店卖的电脑很好。我们吃饭后去看看吧。

爸爸：今天我不能去商店。我们过几天去吧。

我：不能过几天去。我们明天去好不好？

爸爸：明天我去工作，也不能去啊。

我：明天下午怎么样？

爸爸：你先去商店看看哪个电脑好，卖多少钱。过几天我和你一起去买吧。

我：好吧。

明天在学校里，老师听见我爸爸很不高兴，老师就说：

老师：我听说你爸爸很不高兴我叫你去买电脑，是吗？

我：是的。对不起，老师。我爸爸是这样的。

老师：没关系。那你几时能有电脑呢？

我：昨天爸爸叫我先去商店看看哪个电脑好。我也不能说我几时能买到电脑。

老师：你爸爸为什么不高兴你买电脑呢？

我：他说买电脑用很多钱。叫我看书不用买电脑了。

老师：如果是因为钱，我看你能买这个电脑，因为学校多买了一个电脑。这个电脑也不是很多钱。

我：太谢谢您了，老师。我看我爸爸会让我买这个电脑的。我很高兴能买到电脑了！

Pinyin and Translation [2]

在学校里有很多人会用电脑。我和同学们都会用电脑。可是家里的爸爸妈妈就不会用电脑。老师让我问爸爸妈妈能不能买个电脑在家里用。昨天爸爸出去的时候在下雨，他回到家的时候很不高兴，我就没问他能不能买电脑了。

Zài xuéxiào li yǒu hěnduō rén huì yòng diànnǎo. Wǒ hé tóngxuémen dōu huì yòng diànnǎo. Kěshì jiālǐ de bàba māmā jiù bù huì yòng diànnǎo. Lǎoshī ràng wǒ wèn bàba māmā néng bùnéng mǎi gè diànnǎo zài jiālǐ yòng. Zuótiān bàba chūqù de shíhòu zàixià yǔ, tā huí dàojiā de shíhòu hěn bù gāoxìng, wǒ jiù méi wèn tā néng bùnéng mǎi diànnǎole.

There are many people in school who can use the computer. My classmates and I can use the computer. But Mom and Dad can't use the computer. The teacher told me to ask Mum and Dad to buy a computer to use at home. It rained when my Dad went out yesterday, and he was very unhappy when he got home. That day, I didn't ask him if I could buy a computer.

今天他看来是高兴一点儿。这是因为他的汉语老师说他写的字很好。他回到家的时候就叫我们一起去饭馆吃饭了。

Jīntiān tā kàn lái shì gāoxìng yīdiǎn er. Zhè shì yīnwèi tā de hànyǔ lǎoshī shuō tā xiě de zì hěn hǎo. Tā huí dàojiā de shíhòu jiù jiào wǒmen yīqǐ qù fànguǎn chīfànle.

Today he seems to be a little happier. This is because his Chinese teacher said he wrote very well. When he got home, he told us to go to the restaurant for dinner.

在饭馆里:

Zài fànguǎn lǐ:

In the restaurant:

我：爸爸，老师让我问你能不能买个电脑在家里用。因为学校里的电脑很少，太多同学们用电脑了。如果家里有个电脑，我就能在家里学习和写字了。

Wǒ: Bàba, lǎoshī ràng wǒ wèn nǐ néng bùnéng mǎi gè diànnǎo zài jiālǐ yòng. Yīn wéi xuéxiào lǐ de diànnǎo hěn shǎo, tài duō tóngxuémen yòng diànnǎole. Rúguǒ jiā li yǒu gè diànnǎo, wǒ jiù néng zài jiālǐ xuéxí hé xiězìle.

Me: Dad, the teacher asked me if you could buy a computer for home use. Because there are very few computers in the school and too many students are using the computers. If I have a computer at home, I would be able to write and study at home.

爸爸：为什么用电脑学习和写字呢？你不是用书吗？

Bàba: Wèishéme yòng diànnǎo xuéxí hé xiězì ní? Nǐ bùshì yòngshū ma?

Dad: Why use computers to learn and write? Are you not using books?

我：用电脑来写字会写的快点儿，学习也会学的快点儿。

Wǒ: Yòng diànnǎo lái xiězì huì xiě de kuài diǎn er, xuéxí yě huì xué de kuài diǎn er.

Me: I will write faster when I use a computer to write. I will also learn more quickly.

爸爸：是吗？我在学习汉语时也没用电脑。我的老师也没叫我买电脑。我不是买了很多书给你吗？

Bàba: Shì ma? Wǒ zài xuéxí hànyǔ shí yě méi yòng diànnǎo. Wǒ de lǎoshī yě méi jiào wǒ mǎi diànnǎo. Wǒ bùshì mǎile hěnduō shū gěi nǐ ma?

Dad: Is it? I didn't use a computer when I was learning Chinese. My teacher didn't ask me to buy a computer. Didn't I buy a lot of books for you?

我：是啊爸爸，你买了很多书给我，但是只用书是不能的。学校里，同学们都用电脑，我的老师也用电脑。我怎么能不用电脑呢？

Wǒ: Shì a bàba, nǐ mǎile hěnduō shū gěi wǒ, dànshì zhǐ yòngshū shì bùnéng de. Xuéxiào lǐ, tóngxuémen dōu yòng diànnǎo, wǒ de lǎoshī yě yòng diànnǎo. Wǒ zěnme néng bùyòng diànnǎo ne?

Me: Yes, Dad, you bought a lot of books for me, but I can't use books alone. In school, students use computers, and my teachers use computers. How can I not use a computer?

爸爸：我看你的学校和老师是多做的。

Bàba: Wǒ kàn nǐ de xuéxiào hé lǎoshī shì duō zuò de.

Dad: I think your school and teachers have nothing better to do.

我：不是啊。很多同学的家里已经有电脑了。如果我们不买电脑，就会很难学习，因为别的同学会比我学的快。

Wǒ: Bùshì a. Hěnduō tóngxué de jiālǐ yǐjīng yǒu diànnǎole. Rúguǒ wǒmen bú mǎi diànnǎo, jiù huì hěn nán xuéxí, yīnwèi bié de tóngxué huì bǐ wǒ xué de kuài.

Me: No. Many students have computers at home. If we don't buy a computer, it will be difficult for me to learn, because other students will learn faster than I can.

爸爸：我用书来学习，没用电脑，我不还是学的很快吗。你为什么不能？

Bàba: Wǒ yòngshū lái xuéxí, méi yòng diànnǎo, wǒ bù háishì xué de hěn kuài ma. Nǐ wèishéme bùnéng?

Dad: I use books to learn, no computer, I still learn very quickly. Why can't you?

我：爸爸，我怎么样说你才会买电脑给我呢？

Wǒ: Bàba, wǒ zěnme yàng shuō nǐ cái huì mǎi diànnǎo gěi wǒ ne?

Me: Dad, what do I have to say so that you will buy me a computer?

爸爸：买电脑用很多钱的。你就用书来学习吧。

Bàba: Mǎi diànnǎo yòng hěnduō qián de. Nǐ jiù yòngshū lái xuéxí ba.

Dad: It costs a lot of money to buy a computer. You just use books to learn.

我：我有一个同学，他买电脑不是用了很多钱。他说有一个商店卖的电脑很好。我们吃饭后去看看吧。

Wǒ: Wǒ yǒu yīgè tóngxué, tā mǎi diànnǎo bùshì yòngle hěnduō qián. Tā shuō yǒu yīgè shāngdiàn mài de diànnǎo hěn hǎo. Wǒmen chīfàn hòu qù kàn kàn ba.

Me: I have a classmate who didn’t use a lot of money to buy a computer. He said there is a shop that sells very good computers. Let's go and have a look after dinner.

爸爸：今天我不能去商店。我们过几天去吧。

Bàba: Jīntiān wǒ bùnéng qù shāngdiàn. Wǒmenguò jǐ tiān qù ba.

Dad: I can't go to the store today. Let's go in a few days’ time.

我：不能过几天去。我们明天去好不好?

Wǒ: Bùnéngguò jǐ tiān qù. Wǒmen míngtiān qù hǎobù hǎo?

Me: It can't be in a few days. Can we go tomorrow?

爸爸：明天我去工作，也不能去啊。

Bàba: Míngtiān wǒ qù gōngzuò, yě bùnéng qù a.

Dad: I'm going to work tomorrow, and I can't go.

我：明天下午怎么样？

Wǒ: Míngtiān xiàwǔ zěnme yàng?

Me: How about tomorrow afternoon?

爸爸：你先去商店看看哪个电脑好，卖多少钱。过几天我和你一起去买吧。

Bàba: Nǐ xiān qù shāngdiàn kàn kàn nǎge diànnǎo hǎo, mài duōshǎo qián.Guò jǐ tiān wǒ hé nǐ yīqǐ qù mǎi ba.

Dad: You go to the store first to see which computer is good and how much is it selling for. I'll go and buy it with you in a few days.

我：好吧。

Wǒ: Hǎo ba.

Me: Ok.

明天在学校里，老师听见我爸爸很不高兴，老师就说：

Míngtiān zài xuéxiào lǐ, lǎoshī tīngjiàn wǒ bàba hěn bù gāoxìng, lǎoshī jiù shuō:

The next day at school, the teacher heard that my Dad was very upset, and the teacher said:

老师：我听说你爸爸很不高兴我叫你去买电脑，是吗？

Lǎoshī: Wǒ tīng shuō nǐ bàba hěn bù gāoxìng wǒ jiào nǐ qù mǎi diànnǎo, shì ma?

Teacher: I heard your Dad was upset that I told you to buy a computer, is it?

我：是的。对不起，老师。我爸爸是这样的。

Wǒ: Shì de. Duìbùqǐ, lǎoshī. Wǒ bàba shì zhèyàng de.

Me: Yes. I'm sorry, sir. My Dad is like that.

老师：没关系。那你几时能有电脑呢？

Lǎoshī: Méiguānxì. Nà nǐ jǐshí néng yǒu diànnǎo ne?

Teacher: It doesn't matter. Then when can you have a computer?

我：昨天爸爸叫我先去商店看看哪个电脑好。我也不能说我几时能买到电脑。

Wǒ: Zuótiān bàba jiào wǒ xiān qù shāngdiàn kàn kàn nǎge diànnǎo hǎo. Wǒ yě bùnéng shuō wǒ jǐshí néng mǎi dào diànnǎo.

Me: Yesterday, Dad told me to go to the store to see which computer is good. I can't say when I can buy a computer.

老师：你爸爸为什么不高兴你买电脑呢？

Lǎoshī: Nǐ bàba wèishéme bù gāoxìng nǐ mǎi diànnǎo ne?

Teacher: Why is your Dad not happy with you wanting to buy a computer?

我：他说买电脑用很多钱。叫我看书不用买电脑了。

Wǒ: Tā shuō mǎi diànnǎo yòng hěnduō qián. Jiào wǒ kànshū bùyòng mǎi diànnǎole.

Me: He said that buying a computer costs a lot of money. Asked me to read books instead of buying a computer.

老师：如果是因为钱，我看你能买这个电脑，因为学校多买了一个电脑。这个电脑也不是很多钱。

Lǎoshī: Rúguǒ shì yīnwèi qián, wǒ kàn nǐ néng mǎi zhège diànnǎo, yīn wéi xuéxiào duō mǎile yīgè diànnǎo. Zhège diànnǎo yě bùshì hěnduō qián.

Teacher: If it is because of money, I think you can buy this computer because the school bought an extra computer. This computer does not cost a lot of money.

我：太谢谢您了，老师。我看我爸爸会让我买这个电脑的。我很高兴能买到电脑了！

Wǒ: Tài xièxiè nínle, lǎoshī. Wǒ kàn wǒ bàba huì ràng wǒ mǎi zhège diànnǎo de. Wǒ hěn gāoxìng néng mǎi dào diànnǎole!

Me: Thank you so much, teacher. I think my Dad will let me buy this computer. I am very happy that I can buy a computer!

Statistics for Story [3]

602 Total Word Count

110 Number of Unique Words

70 (46.67 %) of the 150 HSK 1 words are used in this Story

89.7 % of the Story comprise of the Extended HSK 1 words

20 New Words

New Words	Pinyin	Explanation
还	hái	Also, still, yet
就	jiù	at once, right away, as soon as, then, in that case
它	tā	It
过	guò	Over, cross, pass (time)
如果	rú guǒ	If, in case, in the event that
天天	tiān tiān	Everyday
走	zǒu	To walk, to go
只	zhǐ	Only, merely, just, classifier for dogs, cats, birds and certain animals

New Words	Pinyin	Explanation
所以	suǒ yǐ	Therefore, as a result, so, the reason why
鱼	yú	Fish
已经	yǐjīng	Already, have
对	duì	To, at
到	dào	Arrive, up to (verb complement denoting completion or result of an action)
可是	kěshì	But, however
再	zài	Again
着	zhe	aspect particle indicating action in progress for e.g looking at (看着)
用	yòng	use
才	cái	Only
见	jiàn	See, meet
快	kuài	Fast, quickly, soon

[3] What Do Kittens Eat?

小猫吃什么？

昨天上午在学校里，我听见三个同学在说话：

同学一：你有没有看见那只小猫？

同学二：哪只小猫？我没看见。

同学一：它天天都来这儿的。我天天都给它米饭吃。

同学三：小猫不吃米饭的，它喜欢吃鱼。

同学二：谁说的？不是。小猫喜欢吃水果。

同学一：哪的猫会吃水果啊？我没听过。

同学二：你没听过？我妈妈说过猫很爱吃苹果的。

同学三：我有听过狗会吃苹果可是没听过猫会吃什么水果。我爸爸天天都给我家里的猫吃鱼。爸爸说吃鱼对猫的身体很好。

同学一：不是。米饭对猫的身体很好。我天天都给这里的小猫吃米饭。

同学二：我这儿有些苹果，给你，如果你看见小猫就给小猫吧。

同学一：我什么水果都不会给小猫吃的。你不用给我苹果了。

同学二：我也是想小猫的身体好一点儿，所以给它吃点儿苹果。如果你不想给猫吃，我就不给你了。

同学三：你给我吧。我想吃苹果。

同学二：你是不是想吃苹果所以你说猫不喜欢吃苹果？

同学三：我是这样的人吗？

同学一：我没想什么。只想看见那只小猫。

同学二：好了，好了。我给你这个苹果。我不给猫吃了，你就好好吃吧。

同学三：我上午没吃什么，所以现在想吃东西。也想喝水。你有水吗？

同学一：你为什么想这么多东西的？我这儿还有些米饭。都给你好吗？

同学三：好。太谢谢你了。

同学一：不客气。今天我妈妈会做很多菜的。你想不想来我家吃饭？

同学二：你为什么不叫我去你的家吃饭？

同学一：好啊。你也一起来我家吃饭吧。

同学三：如果我们现在走了，小猫就没东西吃了。

同学二：我们在这儿多几分钟吧。如果小猫还不来，我们才走。

同学一：好，就这样吧。

三十分钟后：

同学二：我们已经在这儿多三十分钟了，还没看见小猫。我们能不能现在去你家吃饭？

同学三：我们还是走吧。我看小猫不会来的。

同学一：好吧。我们现在就走。

同学二：我们怎么样去你家呢？

同学一：我们打出租车去。你看！小猫来了！快点儿给它米饭吃。

同学三：对不起。没有米饭了。我已经吃了。

同学一：什么？那小猫今天没东西吃了。

同学二：我还有苹果。

同学一很不高兴的看着同学三说：“吃饭后我们回到这儿给小猫米饭吃吧。”

同学三：猫不吃米饭的。吃水果的。我们还有苹果，给它苹果吃吧。

同学二：你还再说？你想不想去他的家吃饭啊。

Pinyin and Translation [3]

昨天上午在学校里我听见三个同学在说话:

Zuótiān shàngwǔ zài xuéxiào lǐ wǒ tīngjiàn sān gè tóngxué zài shuōhuà:

I heard three classmates talking in school yesterday morning:

同学一:你有没有看见那只小猫?

Tóngxué yī: Nǐ yǒu méiyǒu kànjiàn nà zhǐ xiǎo māo?

Classmate 1: Have you seen the kitten?

同学二:哪只小猫?我没看见。

Tóngxué èr: Nǎ zhǐ xiǎo māo? Wǒ méi kànjiàn.

Classmate 2: Which kitten? I don't see it.

同学一:它天天都来这儿的。我天天都给它米饭吃。

Tóngxué yī: Tā tiāntiān dōu lái zhè'er de. Wǒ tiāntiān dū gěi tā mǐ fàn chī.

Classmate 1: It comes here every day. I give it rice every day.

同学三：小猫不吃米饭的，它喜欢吃鱼。

Tóngxué sān: Xiǎo māo bù chī mǐfàn de, tā xǐhuān chī yú.

Classmate 3: The kitten does not eat rice. It likes to eat fish.

同学二：谁说的？不是。小猫喜欢吃水果。

Tóngxué èr: Shéi shuō de? Bùshì. Xiǎo māo xǐhuān chī shuǐguǒ.

Classmate 2: Who said that? No. Kittens like to eat fruit.

同学一：哪的猫会吃水果啊？我没听过。

Tóngxué yī: Nǎ'er de māo huì chī shuǐguǒ a? Wǒ méi tīngguò.

Classmate 1: Which cat eat fruits? I have not heard of it.

同学二：你没听过？我妈妈说过猫很爱吃苹果的。

Tóngxué èr: Nǐ méi tīngguò? Wǒ māmā shuōguò māo hěn ài chī píngguǒ de.

Classmate 2: You haven't heard of it? My Mom said that cats love apples.

同学三：我有听过狗会吃苹果可是没听过猫会吃什么水果。我爸爸天天都给我家里的猫吃鱼。爸爸说吃鱼对猫的身体很好。

Tóngxué sān: Wǒ yǒu tīngguò gǒu huì chī píngguǒ kěshì méi tīngguò māo huì chī shénme shuǐguǒ. Wǒ bàba tiāntiān dōu gěi wǒ jiālǐ de māo chī yú. Bàba shuō chī yú duì māo de shēntǐ hěn hǎo.

Classmate 3: I have heard of dogs eating apples but have never heard of what fruit a cat will eat. My Dad feeds our family cat with fish every day. Dad said fish is good for the cat's health.

同学一：不是。米饭对猫的身体很好。我天天都给这里的小猫吃米饭。

Tóngxué yī: Bùshì. Mǐfàn duì māo de shēntǐ hěn hǎo. Wǒ tiāntiān dū gěi zhèlǐ de xiǎo māo chī mǐfàn.

Classmate 1: No. Rice is good for cats. I give rice to the kitten here every day.

同学二：我这儿有些苹果，给你，如果你看见小猫就给小猫吧。

Tóngxué èr: Wǒ zhè'er yǒuxiē píngguǒ, gěi nǐ, rúguǒ nǐ kànjiàn xiǎo māo jiù gěi xiǎo māo ba.

Classmate 2: I have some apples here for you, if you see the kitten, give it to the kitten.

同学一：我什么水果都不会给小猫吃的。你不用给我苹果了。

Tóngxué yī: Wǒ shénme shuǐguǒ dōu bù huì gěi xiǎo māo chī de. Nǐ bùyòng gěi wǒ píngguǒle.

Classmate 1: I will not feed any fruit to the kitten. You don't have to give me apples.

同学二：我也是想小猫的身体好一点儿，所以给它吃点儿苹果。如果你不想给猫吃，我就不给你了。

Tóngxué èr: Wǒ yěshì xiǎng xiǎo māo de shēntǐ hǎo yīdiǎn er, suǒyǐ gěi tā chī diǎn er píngguǒ. Rúguǒ nǐ bùxiǎng gěi māo chī, wǒ jiù bù gěi nǐle.

Classmate 2: I also want the kitten to be healthier, so give it some apples. If you won’t feed the cat, I won't give it to you then.

同学三：你给我吧。我想吃苹果。

Tóngxué sān: Nǐ gěi wǒ ba. Wǒ xiǎng chī píngguǒ.

Classmate 3: Give it to me. I want to eat apples.

同学二：你是不是想吃苹果所以你说猫不喜欢吃苹果？

Tóngxué èr: Nǐ shì bùshì xiǎng chī píngguǒ suǒyǐ nǐ shuō māo bù xǐhuān chī píngguǒ?

Classmate 2: You want to eat apples so you said cats don't like apples?

同学三：我是这样的人吗？

Tóngxué sān: Wǒ shì zhèyàng de rén ma?

Classmate 3: Am I such a person?

同学一：我没想什么。只想看见那只小猫。

Tóngxué yī: Wǒ méi xiǎng shénme. Zhǐ xiǎng kànjiàn nà zhǐ xiǎo māo.

Classmate 1: I didn't think about anything else. I just want to see the kitten.

同学二：好了，好了。我给你这个苹果。我不给猫吃了，你就好好吃吧。

Tóngxué èr: Hǎole, hǎole. Wǒ gěi nǐ zhège píngguǒ. Wǒ bù gěi māo chīle, nǐ jiù hǎo hào chī ba.

Classmate 2: Ok, well. I will give you this apple. I won’t feed the kitten, you just eat it.

同学三：我上午没吃什么，所以现在想吃东西。也想喝水。你有水吗？

Tóngxué sān: Wǒ shàngwǔ méi chī shénme, suǒyǐ xiànzài xiǎng chī dōngxī. Yě xiǎng hē shuǐ. Nǐ yǒu shuǐ ma?

Classmate 3: I didn't eat anything in the morning, so I want to eat something now. I also want to drink water. Do you have water?

同学一：你为什么想这么多东西的？我这儿还有些米饭。都给你好吗？

Tóngxué yī: Nǐ wèishéme xiǎng zhème duō dōngxī de? Wǒ zhè'er hái yǒuxiē mǐfàn. Dōu gěi nǐ hǎo ma?

Classmate 1: Why do you want so many things? I still have some rice here. I'll give it to you, ok?

同学三：好。太谢谢你了。

Tóngxué sān: Hǎo. Tài xièxiè nǐle.

Classmate 3: Good. Thank you so much.

同学一：不客气。今天我妈妈会做很多菜的。你想不想来我家吃饭？

Tóngxué yī: Bù kèqì. Jīntiān wǒ māmā huì zuò hěnduō cài de. Nǐ xiǎng bùxiǎng lái wǒjiā chīfàn?

Classmate 1: You are welcome. Today my Mom will cook a lot of dishes. Do you want to come to my house to eat?

同学二：你为什么不叫我去你的家吃饭？

Tóngxué èr: Nǐ wèishéme bù jiào wǒ qù nǐ de jiā chīfàn?

Classmate 2: Why didn't you ask me to go to your house to eat?

同学一：好啊。你也一起来我家吃饭吧。

Tóngxué yī: Hǎo a. Nǐ yě yī qǐlái wǒjiā chīfàn ba.

Classmate 1: OK. You can come to my house for dinner, too.

同学三：如果我们现在走了，小猫就没东西吃了。

Tóngxué sān: Rúguǒ wǒmen xiànzài zǒule, xiǎo māo jiù méi dōngxī chīle.

Classmate 3: If we go now, the kitten will have nothing to eat.

同学二：我们在这儿多几分钟吧。如果小猫还不来，我们才走。

Tóngxué èr: Wǒmen zài zhè'er duō jǐ fēnzhōng ba. Rúguǒ xiǎo māo hái bù lái, wǒmen cái zǒu.

Classmate 2: Let's stay here for a few more minutes. If the kitten still doesn't come, then we go.

同学一：好，就这样吧。

Tóngxué yī: Hǎo, jiù zhèyàng ba.

Classmate 1: OK, let's do this.

三十分钟后：

Sānshí fēnzhōng hòu:

After 30 minutes:

同学二：我们已经在这儿多三十分钟了，还没看见小猫。我们能不能现在去你家吃饭？

Tóngxué èr: Wǒmen yǐjīng zài zhè'er duō sānshí fēnzhōngle, hái méi kànjiàn xiǎo māo. Wǒmen néng bùnéng xiànzài qù nǐ jiā chīfàn?

Classmate 2: We have been here for more than 30 minutes, and have not seen the kitten. Can we go to your home to eat now?

同学三：我们还是走吧。我看小猫不会来的。

Tóngxué sān: Wǒmen háishì zǒu ba. Wǒ kàn xiǎo māo bù huì lái de.

Classmate 3: Let's go. I don't think the kitten will come.

同学一：好吧。我们现在就走。

Tóngxué yī: Hǎo ba. Wǒmen xiànzài jiù zǒu.

Classmate 1: Ok. Let's go now.

同学二：我们怎么样去你家呢？

Tóngxué èr: Wǒmen zěnme yàng qù nǐ jiā ne?

Classmate 2: How do we get to your house?

同学一：我们打出租车去。你看！小猫来了！快点儿给它米饭吃。

Tóngxué yī: Wǒmen dǎ chūzū chē qù. Nǐ kàn! Xiǎo māo láile! Kuài diǎn er gěi tā mǐ fàn chī.

Classmate 1: Let's take a taxi. You see! Here comes the kitten! Give it some rice quickly.

同学三：对不起。没有米饭了。我已经吃了。

Tóngxué sān: Duìbùqǐ. Méiyǒu mǐfànle. Wǒ yǐjīng chīle.

Classmate 3: I'm sorry. There's no rice. I've already finished it.

同学一：什么？那小猫今天没东西吃了。

Tóngxué yī: Shénme? Nà xiǎo māo jīntiān méi dōngxī chīle.

Classmate 1: What? Then the kitten has nothing to eat today.

同学二：我还有苹果。

Tóngxué èr: Wǒ hái yǒu píngguǒ.

Classmate 2: I still have apples.

同学一很不高兴的看着同学三说："吃饭后我们回到这儿给小猫米饭吃吧。"

Tóngxué yī hěn bù gāoxìng de kànzhe tóngxué sān shuō:"Chīfàn hòu wǒmen huí dào zhè'er gěi xiǎo māo mǐ fàn chī ba."

Classmate 1 was very upset, glared at Classmate 3 and said: "After our meal, we will return here to feed the kitten some rice."

同学三：猫不吃米饭的。吃水果的。我们还有苹果，给它苹果吃吧。

Tóngxué sān: Māo bù chī mǐfàn de. Chī shuǐguǒ de. Wǒmen hái yǒu píngguǒ, gěi tā píngguǒ chī ba.

Classmate 3: The kitten does not eat rice. Eat fruits. We still have apples, let it have some apples.

同学二：你还再说？你想不想去他的家吃饭啊。

Tóngxué èr: Nǐ hái zàishuō? Nǐ xiǎng bùxiǎng qù tā de jiā chīfàn a.

Classmate 2: Are you still saying that? Do you want to go to his house for dinner or not?

Statistics for Story [4]

620 Total Word Count

127 Number of Unique Words

83 (55.33 %) of the 150 HSK 1 words are used in this Story

88.39 % of the Story comprise of the Extended HSK 1 words

20 New Words

New Words	Pinyin	Explanation
要	yào	Want
就	jiù	at once, right away, as soon as, then, in that case
还	hái	Also, still, yet
因为	yīnwèi	Because, since, for
快	kuài	Fast, quickly, soon
走	zǒu	To walk, to go
找	zhǎo	Find, look for, seek
到	dào	Arrive, up to (verb complement denoting completion or result of an action)

New Words	Pinyin	Explanation
用	yòng	use
时间	shíjiān	Time
可是	kěshì	But, however
已经	yǐjīng	Already, have
才	cái	Only
再	zài	Again
如果	rú guǒ	If, in case, in the event that
着	zhe	aspect particle indicating action in progress for e.g looking at (看着)
课	kè	Class
对	duì	To, towards
为了	wèile	In order to, so as to, because of

[4] I Am Not Taking the Plane

不想坐飞机

学生一：老师，您怎么了？

老师：我没什么。

学生二：老师，请坐下。

学生一：杯子在哪儿？快点儿，给老师一杯茶。

学生三：老师，要不要我叫医生来看看你？

老师：不用了。谢谢。我坐一下就会好了。

学生一：我妈妈在医院工作的。我打个电话给她问一问医生现在能看你吗。

老师：你看，我还能走。我看是因为上午没吃什么东西。

学生二：老师，请坐下来吧。我去买点儿东西给您吃，好不好？

学生三：商店开了吗？

学生一：已经开了。我和你一起去买？

学生二：不用了。你在这儿看着老师吧。

老师：你能不能买一点儿水？

学生二：好吧。

学生二对学生三说：你有没有钱？

学生三：为什么？

学生二：昨天下午，我和几个朋友去看电影。看了电影后，我们去饭馆吃了很多菜和米饭。我用了很多钱，我现在没有钱了。

学生三：我有点儿钱。给你吧。你买了就快点儿回来。

老师：我看我还是回家吧。

学生一：你还没吃什么东西呢。

学生二：回来了。老师，吃点儿吧。

老师：我想喝点儿水。

学生三：你昨天看什么电影？好看吗？

学生二：不是很好看。是说有个人不喜欢坐飞机，为了不要坐飞机，他那天就没去工作了。很多人找他都找不到。飞机要飞的时候，他的朋友才找到他。可是他还是不要上飞机。。。

老师：我想回家睡觉。我看我今天不能上课了。

学生一：老师，您打出租车吧，不要开车。

老师：好吧，你。。。。

老师二：你在这儿！我们在找你。飞机要起飞了，你还在这儿。快点儿走吧。我们没有时间了。

学生一：可是老师要回家睡觉。他上午没吃什么东西。我们才买了点儿东西给老师吃。

老师二：他不是没吃东西，他是吃不下，因为下午我们要坐飞机去北京工作了。我们会在北京七个月。他不要坐飞机，因为他不喜欢坐飞机。

老师：我不是不要，我是不能坐飞机。一听到要坐飞机这几个字，我就会这样了。对不起。

老师二：没关系。你为什么不喜欢坐飞机呢？很多人要坐飞机都不能，因为没有钱。我们快点儿走吧。

学生三：老师，您为什么不喜欢坐飞机呢？我很喜欢坐飞机！

老师：我就是不喜欢，没为什么的。一听到要坐飞机，我就不能吃，不能睡觉了。我已经好几天没睡觉了。

老师二：我们还是走吧，我开车。没有时间了，不要再说这么多。

老师：好吧。如果你开车去，谁会开你的车回来？

老师二：我有一个朋友在那儿工作。他会开我的车回来。

老师：学生们，再见了。不要太想我了。

学生们说：老师，再见了。您要好好坐飞机。

Pinyin and Translation [4]

学生一：老师，您怎么了？

Xuéshēng yī: Lǎoshī, nín zěnmele?

Student 1: Teacher, what happened to you?

老师：我没什么。

Lǎoshī: Wǒ méishénme.

Teacher: I am ok.

学生二：老师，请坐下。

Xuéshēng èr: Lǎoshī, qǐng zuò xià.

Student 2: Teacher, please have a seat.

学生一：杯子在哪儿？快点儿，给老师一杯茶。

Xuéshēng yī: Bēizi zài nǎ'er? Kuài diǎn er, gěi lǎoshī yībēi chá.

Student 1: Where is the cup? Hurry up, give the teacher a cup of tea.

学生三：老师，要不要我叫医生来看看你？

Xuéshēng sān: Lǎoshī, yào bùyào wǒ jiào yīshēng lái kàn kàn nǐ?

Student 3: Teacher, do you want me to call a doctor to check on you?

老师：不用了。谢谢。我坐一下就会好了。

Lǎoshī: Bùyòngle. Xièxiè. Wǒ zuò yīxià jiù huì hǎole.

Teacher: No, no. Thank you. I will sit down for awhile and I will be fine.

学生一：我妈妈在医院工作的。我打个电话给她问一问医生现在能看你吗。

Xuéshēng yī: Wǒ māmā zài yīyuàn gōngzuò de. Wǒ dǎ gè diànhuà gěi tā wèn yī wèn yīshēng xiànzài néng kàn nǐ ma.

Student 1: My mother works in the hospital. I will call her and ask if the doctor can see you now.

老师：你看，我还能走。我看是因为上午没吃什么东西。

Lǎoshī: Nǐ kàn, wǒ hái néng zǒu. Wǒ kàn shì yīn wéi shàngwǔ méi chī shénme dōngxī.

Teacher: Look, I can still get up. I think it is because I didn't have anything to eat in the morning.

学生二：老师，请坐下来吧。我去买点儿东西给您吃，好不好？

Xuéshēng èr: Lǎoshī, qǐng zuò xiàlái ba. Wǒ qù mǎidiǎn er dōngxī gěi nín chī, hǎobù hǎo?

Student 2: Teacher, please sit down. I am going to buy you something to eat, ok?

学生三：商店开了吗？

Xuéshēng sān: Shāngdiàn kāile ma?

Student 3: Is the store open?

学生一：已经开了。我和你一起去买？

Xuéshēng yī: Yǐjīng kāile. Wǒ hé nǐ yīqǐ qù mǎi?

Student 1: It is open. I will go with you?

学生二：不用了。你在这儿看着老师吧。

Xuéshēng èr: Bùyòngle. Nǐ zài zhè'er kànzhe lǎoshī ba.

Student 2: No need. Stay here and look after the teacher.

老师：你能不能买一点儿水？

Lǎoshī: Nǐ néng bùnéng mǎi yīdiǎn er shuǐ?

Teacher: Can you buy some water?

学生二：好吧。

Xuéshēng èr: Hǎo ba.

Student 2: Ok.

学生二对学生三说：你有没有钱？

Xuéshēng èr duì xuéshēng sān shuō: Nǐ yǒu méiyǒu qián?

Student 2 said to Student 3: Do you have any money?

学生三：为什么？

Xuéshēng sān: Wèishéme?

Student 3: Why?

学生二：昨天下午，我和几个朋友去看电影。看了电影后，我们去饭馆吃了很多菜和米饭。我用了很多钱，我现在没有钱了。

Xuéshēng èr: Zuótiān xiàwǔ, wǒ hé jǐ gè péngyǒu qù kàn diànyǐng. Kànle diànyǐng hòu, wǒmen qù fànguǎn chīle hěnduō cài hé mǐfàn. Wǒ yòngle hěnduō qián, wǒ xiànzài méiyǒu qiánle.

Student 2: Yesterday afternoon, I went to the movies with a few friends. After watching the movie, we went to the restaurant and ate a lot of rice and dishes. I used a lot of money, I have no money now.

学生三：我有点儿钱。给你吧。你买了就快点儿回来。

Xuéshēng sān: Wǒ yǒudiǎn er qián. Gěi nǐ ba. Nǐ mǎile jiù kuài diǎn er huílái.

Student 3: I have some money. Here you go. Come back soon after you buy it.

老师：我看我还是回家吧。

Lǎoshī: Wǒ kàn wǒ háishì huí jiā ba.

Teacher: I think I may as well go home.

学生一：你还没吃什么东西呢。

Xuéshēng yī: Nǐ hái méi chī shénme dōngxī ne.

Student 1: You haven't eaten anything yet.

学生二：回来了。老师，吃点儿吧。

Xuéshēng èr: Huíláile. Lǎoshī, chī diǎn er ba.

Student 2: He is back. Teacher, have some food.

老师：我想喝点儿水。

Lǎoshī: Wǒ xiǎng hē diǎn er shuǐ.

Teacher: I want to drink some water.

学生三：你昨天看什么电影？好看吗？

Xuéshēng sān: Nǐ zuótiān kàn shénme diànyǐng? Hǎokàn ma?

Student 3: What movie did you watch yesterday? Was it good?

学生二：不是很好看。是说有个人不喜欢坐飞机，为了不要坐飞机，他那天就没去工作了。很多人找他都找不到。飞机要飞的时候，他的朋友才找到他。可是他还是不要上飞机。。。

Xuéshēng èr: Bùshì hěn hǎokàn. Shì shuō yǒu gèrén bù xǐhuān zuò fēijī, wèi le bùyào zuò fēijī, tā nèitiān jiù méi qù gōngzuòle. Hěnduō rén zhǎo tā dōu zhǎo bù dào. Fēijī yào fēi de shíhòu, tā de péngyǒu cái zhǎodào tā. Kěshì tā háishì bùyào shàng fēijī...

Student 2: Not very good. There was a man who doesn't like to fly, so he didn't go to work that day in order not to fly. A lot of people were looking for him. It was only when the plane was about to fly that his friend found him. But he still refuse to get on the plane ...

老师：我想回家睡觉。我看我今天不能上课了。

Lǎoshī: Wǒ xiǎng huí jiā shuìjiào. Wǒ kàn wǒ jīntiān bùnéng shàngkèle.

Teacher: I want to go home and rest. I don’t think I can go to class today.

学生一：老师，您打出租车吧，不要开车。

Xuéshēng yī: Lǎoshī, nín dǎ chūzū chē ba, bùyào kāichē.

Student 1: Teacher, please take a taxi, don't drive.

老师：好吧，你。。。。

Lǎoshī: Hǎo ba, nǐ....

Teacher: Ok, you. . . .

老师二：你在这儿！我们在找你。飞机要起飞了，你还在这儿。快点儿走吧。我们没有时间了。

Lǎoshī èr: Nǐ zài zhè'er! Wǒmen zài zhǎo nǐ. Fēijī yào qǐfēile, nǐ hái zài zhè'er. Kuài diǎn er zǒu ba. Wǒmen méiyǒu shíjiānle.

Teacher 2: You are here! We have been looking for you. The plane is going to take off and you are still here. Let's go. We don't have time.

学生一：可是老师要回家睡觉。他上午没吃什么东西。我们才买了点儿东西给老师吃。

Xuéshēng yī: Kěshì lǎoshī yào huí jiā shuìjiào. Tā shàngwǔ méi chī shénme dōngxī. Wǒmen cái mǎile diǎn er dōngxī gěi lǎoshī chī.

Student 1: But the teacher is going to go home to rest. He didn't eat anything in the morning. We just bought something for the teacher to eat.

老师二：他不是没吃东西，他是吃不下，因为下午我们要坐飞机去北京工作了。我们会在北京七个月。他不要坐飞机，因为他不喜欢坐飞机。

Lǎoshī èr: Tā bùshì méi chī dōngxī, tā shì chī bùxià, yīnwèi xiàwǔ wǒmen yào zuò fēijī qù běijīng gōngzuòle. Wǒmen huì zài běijīng qī gè yuè. Tā bùyào zuò fēijī, yīnwèi tā bù xǐhuān zuò fēijī.

Teacher 2: It is not that he didn’t eat, it is he can't eat, because we are flying to Beijing to work in the afternoon . We will be in

Beijing for 7 months. He does not want to fly because he does not like to fly.

老师：我不是不要，我是不能坐飞机。一听到要坐飞机这几个字，我就会这样了。对不起。

Lǎoshī: Wǒ bùshì bùyào, wǒ shì bùnéng zuò fēijī. Yī tīng dào yào zuò fēijī zhè jǐ gè zì, wǒ jiù huì zhèyàngle. Duìbùqǐ.

Teacher: It is not that I don't want to fly, I can't fly. I will be like this when I hear those words. I am sorry.

老师二：没关系。你为什么不喜欢坐飞机呢？很多人要坐飞机都不能，因为没有钱。我们快点儿走吧。

Lǎoshī èr: Méiguānxì. Nǐ wèishéme bù xǐhuān zuò fēijī ne? Hěnduō rén yào zuò fēijī dōu bùnéng, yīnwèi méiyǒu qián. Wǒmen kuài diǎn er zǒu ba.

Teacher 2: It doesn't matter. Why don't you like to fly? Many people can't fly, because they have no money to fly. Let's hurry.

学生三：老师，您为什么不喜欢坐飞机呢？我很喜欢坐飞机！

Xuéshēng sān: Lǎoshī, nín wèishéme bù xǐhuān zuò fēijī ne? Wǒ hěn xǐhuān zuò fēijī!

Student 3: Teacher, why don't you like to fly? I really like to fly!

老师：我就是不喜欢，没为什么的。一听到要坐飞机，我就不能吃，不能睡觉了。我已经好几天没睡觉了。

Lǎoshī: Wǒ jiùshì bù xǐhuān, méi wèishéme de. Yī tīng dào yào zuò fēijī, wǒ jiù bùnéng chī, bùnéng shuìjiàole. Wǒ yǐjīng hǎo jǐ tiān méi shuìjiàole.

Teacher: I just don't like it, for no apparent reason. I can't eat and can't sleep when I hear that I have to fly. I have not slept for several days.

老师二：我们还是走吧，我开车。没有时间了，不要再说这么多。

Lǎoshī èr: Wǒmen háishì zǒu ba, wǒ kāichē. Méiyǒu shíjiānle, bùyào zàishuō zhème duō.

Teacher 2: Let's go, I will drive. There is no time, don't talk so much.

老师：好吧。如果你开车去，谁会开你的车回来？

Lǎoshī: Hǎo ba. Rúguǒ nǐ kāichē qù, shéi huì kāi nǐ de chē huílái?

Teacher: Ok. If you drive, who will drive your car back?

老师二：我有一个朋友在那儿工作。他会开我的车回来。

Lǎoshī èr: Wǒ yǒu yīgè péngyǒu zài nà'er gōngzuò. Tā huì kāi wǒ de chē huílái.

Teacher 2: I have a friend who works there. He will drive my car back.

老师：学生们，再见了。不要太想我了。

Lǎoshī: Xuéshēngmen, zàijiànle. Bùyào tài xiǎng wǒle.

Teacher: Students, goodbye. Don't miss me too much.

学生们说：老师，再见了。您要好好坐飞机。

Xuéshēngmen shuō: Lǎoshī, zàijiànle. Nín yào hǎohǎo zuò fēijī.

The students said: Teacher, goodbye. Sit tight in the plane !

Statistics for Story [5]

676 Total Word Count

125 Number of Unique Words

85 (56.67 %) of the 150 HSK 1 words are used in this Story

82.25 % of the Story comprise of the Extended HSK 1 words

23 New Words

New Words	Pinyin	Explanation
小亮	Xiǎo Liàng	Name of a person
小喜	Xiǎo Xǐ	Name of a person
小五	Xiǎo Wǔ	Name of a person
就	jiù	At once, right away, as soon as, then, in that case
男朋友	nán péngyǒu	Boyfriend
已经	yǐjīng	Already, have
可是	kěshì	But, however
用	yòng	Use
女朋友	nǚ péngyǒu	Girlfriend

New Words	Pinyin	Explanation
为什么	wèishéme	Why
因为	yīnwèi	Because, since, for
年纪	niánjì	Age
天天	tiān tiān	Everyday
如果	rú guǒ	If, in case, in the event that
比	bǐ	Compare, contrast
快	kuài	Fast, quickly, soon
才	cái	Only
到	dào	Arrive, up to (verb complement denoting completion or result of an action)
再	zài	Again
还	hái	Also, still, yet
过	guò	Over, cross, pass (time)
让	ràng	Let, allow
只	zhǐ	Only, merely, just, classifier for dogs, cats, birds and certain animals

[5] Xiao Wu is My Boyfriend

小五是我的男朋友

小亮：今天几号？

小喜：今天是二十八号。为什么？

小亮：我爸爸还没给我下个月的钱，我现在没有钱了。

小喜：这个月的钱呢？你已经用了吗？

小亮：这个月的钱已经用了。怎么样呢？现在，我没有钱吃饭了。

小喜：没关系。你来我的家吃饭吧。你有了钱后，就请我去饭馆吃饭。

小亮：好。太谢谢你了。

小喜：不客气。你今天做什么？想不想去看电影？

小亮：不想了，我已经没有钱了，在家里看电视吧。

小喜：电视没什么好看的。我有钱，我请你看电影好吗？

小亮：谢谢你。不用了。我去你的家看电视，怎么样？

小喜：好，可是电视没什么看的。我很想去看电影。

小亮：对不起。我也没想到这个月这么快就没有钱了。

小喜：是啊。为什么你这个月用的这么快呢？

小亮：因为我认识了一个女朋友，天天都和她一起去看电影和去饭馆吃饭，用了很多钱。

小喜：你的女朋友不能给你点儿钱吗？下个月你爸爸就给你钱了。

小亮：她现在不在这儿。她已经坐飞机去了北京学习汉语了。

小喜：你的女朋友多少岁？

小亮：她今年十八岁。

小喜：我的男朋友今年二十七岁。

小亮：你的男朋友这么大。

小喜：是的。我已经认识他好几年了。你呢？你认识了你的女朋友多少个月了？

小亮：才一个月。

小喜：才一个月？她会住在北京多少个月？

小亮：三个月。她说她去北京大学学习汉语三个月。她已经会读很多个汉字，可是不会写汉字。你爱你的男朋友吗？

小喜：我们在一起已经好几年了。我很爱他，他也很爱我。可是我的爸爸妈妈不喜欢他。

小亮：为什么你的爸爸妈妈不喜欢他？他的人好吗？

小喜：他的人很好，可是爸爸妈妈说年纪比我大的多，他们就不喜欢了。

小亮：那，你会怎么做呢？

小喜：我也不能做什么，他们就是不听我说。

小亮：你的男朋友叫什么名字？

小喜：他的名字是小五。

小亮：小五？

小喜：他是这样的。你看，你认识他吗？

小亮：我认识这个小五。他是我的同学。可是我只认识他一年。他的人很好。他在大学里很多朋友，也很多老师喜欢他。

小喜：你能不能和我的爸爸妈妈说小五的好吗？我看他们会听你说。

小亮：好啊。你说什么时候，我就去你家吃饭。

小喜：那我就请你天天来我家吃饭了。

小亮：好啊！我没钱吃饭，如果天天去你的家吃饭是太好了！

小喜：可是我看他们会喜欢你多过喜欢小五。

小亮：为什么？因为我的年纪比小五的年纪小吗？

小喜：是的。他们会叫你做我的男朋友。男的朋友来我家吃饭，他们都会叫他们做我的男朋友。就是因为他们这样，我就没有再请男的朋友回家吃饭了。

小亮：没关系。你让我想一想怎么做。

小喜：谢谢你。

小亮：是我谢谢你。如果不是你请我去你家吃饭，我就没饭吃了。

Pinyin and Translation [5]

小亮：今天几号？

Xiǎo Liàng: Jīntiān jǐ hào?

Xiao Liang: What date is it today?

小喜：今天是二十八号。为什么？

Xiǎo Xǐ: Jīntiān shì èrshíbā hào. Wèishéme?

Xiao Xi: Today is the 28th. Why?

小亮：我爸爸还没给我下个月的钱，我现在没有钱了。

Xiǎo Liàng: Wǒ bàba hái méi gěi wǒ xià gè yuè de qián, wǒ xiànzài méiyǒu qiánle.

Xiao Liang: My father hasn't given me the money for next month. I don't have any money right now.

小喜：这个月的钱呢？你已经用了吗？

Xiǎo Xǐ: Zhège yuè de qián ne? Nǐ yǐjīng yòngle ma?

Xiao Xi: What about the money for this month? Have you used it already?

小亮：这个月的钱已经用了。怎么样呢？现在，我没有钱吃饭了。

Xiǎo Liàng: Zhège yuè de qián yǐjīng yòngle. Zěnme yàng ne? Xiànzài, wǒ méiyǒu qián chīfànle.

Xiao Liang: This month's money has been used. How ? Now, I have no money to eat.

小喜：没关系。你来我的家吃饭吧。你有了钱后，就请我去饭馆吃饭。

Xiǎo Xǐ: Méiguānxì. Nǐ lái wǒ de jiā chīfàn ba. Nǐ yǒule qián hòu, jiù qǐng wǒ qù fànguǎn chīfàn.

Xiao Xi: It doesn't matter. Come to my house to eat. After you have the money, you can invite me to go to the restaurant to eat.

小亮：好。太谢谢你了。

Xiǎo Liàng: Hǎo. Tài xièxiè nǐle.

Xiao Liang: Ok. Thank you so much.

小喜：不客气。你今天做什么？想不想去看电影？

Xiǎo Xǐ: Bù kèqì. Nǐ jīntiān zuò shénme? Xiǎng bùxiǎng qù kàn diànyǐng?

Xiao Xi: You are welcome. What are you doing today? Do you want to go to the movies?

小亮：不想了，我已经没有钱了，在家里看电视吧。

Xiǎo Liàng: Bùxiǎngle, wǒ yǐjīng méiyǒu qiánle, zài jiālǐ kàn diànshì ba.

Xiao Liang: I don't want to, I have no money, let's watch TV at home.

小喜：电视没什么好看的。我有钱，我请你看电影好吗？

Xiǎo Xǐ: Diànshì méishénme hǎokàn de. Wǒ yǒu qián, wǒ qǐng nǐ kàn diànyǐng hǎo ma?

Xiao Xi: TV has nothing good to watch. I have money, can I give you a treat?

小亮：谢谢你。不用了。我去你的家看电视，怎么样？

Xiǎo Liàng: Xièxiè nǐ. Bùyòngle. Wǒ qù nǐ de jiā kàn diànshì, zěnme yàng?

Xiao Liang: Thank you. No need. Let's go to your house to watch TV, how about that?

小喜：好，可是电视没什么看的。我很想去看电影。

Xiǎo Xǐ: Hǎo, kěshì diànshì méishénme kàn de. Wǒ hěn xiǎng qù kàn diànyǐng.

Xiao Xi: Ok, but the TV has nothing much to watch. I really want to go to the movies.

小亮：对不起。我也没想到这个月这么快就没有钱了。

Xiǎo Liàng: Duìbùqǐ. Wǒ yě méi xiǎngdào zhège yuè zhème kuài jiù méiyǒu qiánle.

Xiao Liang: Sorry. I did not expect that there would be no money left so soon.

小喜：是啊。为什么你这个月用的这么快呢？

Xiǎo Xǐ: Shì a. Wèishéme nǐ zhège yuè yòng de zhème kuài ne?

Xiao Xi: Yes. Why did you use up so fast this month?

小亮：因为我认识了一个女朋友，天天都和她一起去看电影和去饭馆吃饭，用了很多钱。

Xiǎo Liàng: Yīnwèi wǒ rènshìle yīgè nǚ péngyǒu, tiāntiān dōu hé tā yīqǐ qù kàn diànyǐng hé qù fànguǎn chīfàn, yòngle hěnduō qián.

Xiao Liang: Because I met a girlfriend, went to see the movies and eat at restaurants with her everyday, used a lot of money.

小喜：你的女朋友不能给你点儿钱吗？下个月你爸爸就给你钱了。

Xiǎo Xǐ: Nǐ de nǚ péngyǒu bùnéng gěi nǐ diǎn er qián ma? Xià gè yuè nǐ bàba jiù gěi nǐ qiánle.

Xiao Xi: Can your girlfriend not give you some money? Your Dad will give you money next month.

小亮：她现在不在这儿。她已经坐飞机去了北京学习汉语了。

Xiǎo Liàng: Tā xiànzài bùzài zhè'er. Tā yǐjīng zuò fēijī qùle běijīng xuéxí hànyǔle.

Xiao Liang: She is not here now. She has already flown to Beijing to study Chinese.

小喜：你的女朋友多少岁？

Xiǎo Xǐ: Nǐ de nǚ péngyǒu duōshǎo suì?

Xiao Xi: How old is your girlfriend?

小亮：她今年十八岁。

Xiǎo Liàng: Tā jīnnián shíbā suì.

Xiao Liang: She is 18 years old this year.

小喜：我的男朋友今年二十七岁。

Xiǎo Xǐ: Wǒ de nán péngyǒu jīnnián èrshíqī suì.

Xiao Xi: My boyfriend is 27 years old this year.

小亮：你的男朋友这么大。

Xiǎo Liàng: Nǐ de nán péngyǒu zhème dà.

Xiao Liang: Your boyfriend is so old.

小喜：是的。我已经认识他好几年了。你呢？你认识了你的女朋友多少个月了？

Xiǎo Xǐ: Shì de. Wǒ yǐjīng rènshì tā hǎojǐ niánle. Nǐ ne? Nǐ rènshìle nǐ de nǚ péngyǒu duōshǎo gè yuèle?

Xiao Xi: Yes. I have known him for several years. What about you? How many months have you known your girlfriend?

小亮：才一个月。

Xiǎo Liàng: Cái yīgè yuè.

Xiao Liang: Only 1 month.

小喜：才一个月？她会住在北京多少个月？

Xiǎo xǐ: Cái yīgè yuè? Tā huì zhù zài běijīng duōshǎo gè yuè?

Xiaoxi: Only one month? How many months will she live in Beijing?

小亮：三个月。她说她去北京大学学习汉语三个月。她已经会读很多个汉字，可是不会写汉字。你爱你的男朋友吗？

Xiǎo Liàng: Sān gè yuè. Tā shuō tā qù běijīng dàxué xuéxí hànyǔ sān gè yuè. Tā yǐjīng huì dú hěnduō gè hànzì, kěshì bù huì xiě hànzì. Nǐ ài nǐ de nán péngyǒu ma?

Xiao Liang: Three months. She said she is going to Peking University to study Chinese for three months. She can read many Chinese characters, but she does not know how to write Chinese characters. Do you love your boyfriend?

小喜：我们在一起已经好几年了。我很爱他，他也很爱我。可是我的爸爸妈妈不喜欢他。

Xiǎo Xǐ: Wǒmen zài yīqǐ yǐjīng hǎojǐ niánle. Wǒ hěn ài tā, tā yě hěn ài wǒ. Kěshì wǒ de bàba māmā bù xǐhuān tā.

Xiao Xi: We have been together for several years. I love him very much, and he loves me too. But my Mom and Dad don't like him.

小亮：为什么你的爸爸妈妈不喜欢他？他的人好吗？

Xiǎo Liàng: Wèishéme nǐ de bàba māmā bù xǐhuān tā? Tā de rén hǎo ma?

Xiao Liang: Why didn't your Mom and Dad like him? How is he?

小喜：他的人很好，可是爸爸妈妈说年纪比我大的多，他们就不喜欢了。

Xiǎo Xǐ: Tā de rén hěn hǎo, kěshì bàba māmā shuō niánjì bǐ wǒ dà de duō, tāmen jiù bù xǐhuānle.

Xiao Xi: He is very good, but Mom and Dad said that he is much older than me, they don't like that.

小亮：那，你会怎么做呢？

Xiǎo Liàng: Nà, nǐ huì zěnme zuò ne?

Xiao Liang: Then, what do you do?

小喜：我也不能做什么，他们就是不听我说。

Xiǎo Xī: Wǒ yě bùnéng zuò shénme, tāmen jiùshì bù tīng wǒ shuō.

Xiao Xi: I can't do anything, they just don't listen to me.

小亮：你的男朋友叫什么名字？

Xiǎo Liàng: Nǐ de nán péngyǒu jiào shénme míngzì?

Xiao Liang: What is your boyfriend's name?

小喜：他的名字是小五。

Xiǎo Xī: Tā de míngzì shì Xiǎo Wǔ.

Xiao Xi: His name is Xiao Wu.

小亮：小五？

Xiǎo Liàng: Xiǎo Wǔ?

Xiao Liang: Xiao Wu?

小喜：他是这样的。你看，你认识他吗？

Xiǎo Xī: Tā shì zhèyàng de. Nǐ kàn, nǐ rènshì tā ma?

Xiao Xi: He looks like this. Look, do you know him?

小亮：我认识这个小五。他是我的同学。可是我只认识他一年。他的人很好。他在大学里很多朋友，也很多老师喜欢他。

Xiǎo Liàng: Wǒ rènshì zhège Xiǎo Wǔ. Tā shì wǒ de tóngxué. Kěshì wǒ zhǐ rènshì tā yī nián. Tā de rén hěn hǎo. Tā zài dàxué lǐ hěnduō péngyǒu, yě hěnduō lǎoshī xǐhuān tā.

Xiao Liang: I know this Xiao Wu. He is my classmate. But I have only known him for a year. He is very good. He has many friends in college and many teachers like him.

小喜：你能不能和我的爸爸妈妈说小五的好吗？我看他们会听你说。

Xiǎo Xǐ: Nǐ néng bùnéng hé wǒ de bàba māmā shuō Xiǎo Wǔ de hǎo ma? Wǒ kàn tāmen huì tīng nǐ shuō.

Xiao Xi: Can you tell my Mom and Dad about Xiao Wu? I think they will listen to you.

小亮：好啊。你说什么时候，我就去你家吃饭。

Xiǎo Liàng: Hǎo a. Nǐ shuō shénme shíhòu, wǒ jiù qù nǐ jiā chīfàn.

Xiao Liang: Ok. Just say when, I'll go to your house for dinner.

小喜：那我就请你天天来我家吃饭了。

Xiǎo Xǐ: Nà wǒ jiù qǐng nǐ tiāntiān lái wǒjiā chīfànle.

Xiao Xi: Then I will ask you to come to my house everyday.

小亮：好啊！我没钱吃饭，如果天天去你的家吃饭是太好了！

Xiǎo Liàng: Hǎo a! Wǒ méi qián chīfàn, rúguǒ tiāntiān qù nǐ de jiā chīfàn shì tài hǎole!

Xiao Liang: Ok! I have no money to eat, it will be great to go to your house every day!

小喜：可是我看他们会喜欢你多过喜欢小五。

Xiǎo Xǐ: Kěshì wǒ kàn tāmen huì xǐhuān nǐ duōguò xǐhuān Xiǎo Wǔ.

Xiao Xi: But I think they will like you more than Xiao Wu.

小亮：为什么？因为我的年纪比小五的年纪小吗？

Xiǎo Liàng: Wèishéme? Yīnwèi wǒ de niánjì bǐ Xiǎo Wǔ de niánjì xiǎo ma?

Xiao Liang: Why? Because I am younger than Xiao Wu?

小喜：是的。他们会叫你做我的男朋友。男的朋友来我家吃饭，他们都会叫他们做我的男朋友。就是因为他们这样，我就没有再请男的朋友回家吃饭了。

Xiǎo Xǐ: Shì de. Tāmen huì jiào nǐ zuò wǒ de nán péngyǒu. Nán de péngyǒu lái wǒjiā chīfàn, tāmen dūhuì jiào tāmen zuò wǒ de nán péngyǒu. Jiùshì yīnwèi tāmen zhèyàng, wǒ jiù méiyǒu zài qǐng nán de péngyǒu huí jiā chīfànle.

Xiao Xi: Yes. They will ask you to be my boyfriend. They will ask any male friends who come to my house to be my boyfriend. It is because of them that I have not asked any male friend to come to my house.

小亮：没关系。你让我想一想怎么做。

Xiǎo Liàng: Méiguānxì. Nǐ ràng wǒ xiǎng yī xiǎng zěnme zuò.

Xiao Liang: It doesn't matter. Let me think about what to do it.

小喜：谢谢你。

Xiǎo Xǐ: Xièxiè nǐ.

Xiao Xi: Thank you.

小亮：是我谢谢你。如果不是你请我去你家吃饭，我就没饭吃了。

Xiǎo Liàng: Shì wǒ xièxiè nǐ. Rúguǒ bùshì nǐ qǐng wǒ qù nǐ jiā chīfàn, wǒ jiù méi fàn chīle.

Xiao Liang: I must thank you. If you didn't ask me to go to your house to eat, I would have no food to eat.

Statistics for Story [6]

480 Total Word Count

114 Number of Unique Words

81 (54.0 %) of the 150 HSK 1 words are used in this Story

88.54 % of the Story comprise of the Extended HSK 1 words

17 New Words

New Words	Pinyin	Explanation
小亮	Xiǎo Liàng	Name of a person
小喜	Xiǎo Xǐ	Name of a person
小五	Xiǎo Wǔ	Name of a person
就	jiù	At once, right away, as soon as, then, in that case
已经	yǐjīng	Already, have
天天	tiān tiān	Everyday
如果	rú guǒ	If, in case, in the event that
才	cái	Only

New Words	Pinyin	Explanation
再	zài	Again
还	hái	Also, still, yet
过	guò	Over, cross, pass (time)
出	chū	Out
只	zhǐ	Only, merely, just, classifier for dogs, cats, birds and certain animals
但是	dàn shì	But, however
别	bié	Other, another, don’t
应该	yīnggāi	Should, ought to
先	xiān	Prior, first, in advance

[6] No More Friends

没有朋友了

这几天，天气很冷，也天天下雨。我哪儿都不想去，只想在家里睡觉。前一个星期，同学打电话来叫我去喝茶，我都不去。今天已经五月四号了。什么时候天气才会好一点儿呢？昨天下大雨，但是今天没下雨。明天会再下雨吗？

我已经多少天没出去了？今天是星期六我还是出去吧。如果再不出去，我朋友都会没有了。好，我先打电话给我的好朋友，小亮和小喜，看他们想不想和我一起去看电影。

我：喂。

小亮：喂。

我：这是小亮吗？

小亮：是啊。请问你是谁？

我：我是小五啊。你好吗？

小亮：我很好。你呢？

我：我也很好。我想今天去看电影。你能不能和我一起去看？

小亮：对不起。今天我和爸爸一起去医院看医生，不能去看电影了。

我：那明天怎么样？

小亮：明天我和妈妈去商店买东西也不能去看电影了。

我：没关系。下个星期我再打个电话给你。

小亮不能去，现在我能做什么呢？谁能和我一起看电影呢？我想我还是打个电话给小喜问一问她能不能和我一起去看电影。

我：喂。这是小喜吗？

小喜：是啊。请问你是谁？

我：我是小五啊。你好吗？

小喜：我很好。你呢？

我：今天你能不能和我一起去看电影？我已经打过电话给小亮，他说他今天和爸爸去医院看医生，不能和我一起去看电影。

小喜：对不起。我在工作，不能去看电影。

我：什么？你在工作？

小喜：是啊。已经有一个多月了。

我：那没关系。我们下个星期再看看怎么样？

小喜：下个星期我和小亮一起坐飞机去北京。他没说吗？

我：没关系。再见。

小亮和小喜都不能和我一起去看电影。我就一个人去看电影吧。我已经有几个星期没和他们说话了。他们也没问我想不想一起去北京。我看小亮和小喜是不会再打电话给我的。

我应该多认识几个朋友。如果有几个朋友不能和我看电影，我还有别的朋友能和我一起看电影啊。就这样吧！明天，我就出去多认识几个朋友。

Pinyin and Translation [6]

这几天，天气很冷，也天天下雨。我哪儿都不想去，只想在家里睡觉。前一个星期，同学打电话来叫我去喝茶，我都不去。今天已经五月四号了。什么时候天气才会好一点儿呢？昨天下大雨，但是今天没下雨。明天会再下雨吗？

Zhè jǐ tiān, tiānqì hěn lěng, yě tiān tiānxià yǔ. Wǒ nǎ'er dōu bùxiǎng qù, zhǐ xiǎng zài jiālǐ shuìjiào. Qián yīgè xīngqí, tóngxué dǎ diànhuà lái jiào wǒ qù hē chá, wǒ dū bù qù. Jīntiān yǐjīng wǔ yuè sì hàole. Shénme shíhòu tiānqì cái huì hǎo yīdiǎn er ne? Zuótiān xià dàyǔ, dànshì jīntiān méi xià yǔ. Míngtiān huì zài xià yǔ ma?

The weather is very cold and it has been raining every day. I don't want to go anywhere, I just want to sleep at home. My classmates asked me out for tea but I didn't go. Today is May 4th. When will the weather be better? It was raining yesterday, but it didn't rain today. Will it rain again tomorrow?

我已经多少天没出去了？今天是星期六我还是出去吧。如果再不出去，我朋友都会没有了。好，我先打电话给我的好朋友，小亮和小喜，看他们想不想和我一起去看电影。

Wǒ yǐjīng duōshǎo tiān méi chūqùle? Jīntiān shì xīngqíliù wǒ háishì chūqù ba. Rúguǒ zàibu chūqù, wǒ péngyǒu dūhuì méiyǒule. Hǎo, wǒ xiān dǎ diànhuà gěi wǒ de hǎo péngyǒu, xiǎo liàng hé xiǎo xī, kàn tāmen xiǎng bùxiǎng hé wǒ yīqǐ qù kàn diànyǐng.

How many days have I not gone out? Today is Saturday, I think I should go out. If I don't go out, I will not have any friends left. Ok, I will call my best friends, Xiao Liang and Xiao Xi, and ask if they are interested to go to the movies with me.

我：喂。

Wǒ: Wèi.

Me: Hello.

小亮：喂。

Xiǎo Liàng: Wèi.

Xiao Liang: Hello.

我：这是小亮吗？

Wǒ: Zhè shì Xiǎo Liàng ma?

Me: Is this Xiao Liang?

小亮：是啊。请问你是谁？

Xiǎo Liàng: Shì a. Qǐngwèn nǐ shì shéi?

Xiao Liang: Yes. May I know who am I speaking to?

我：我是小五啊。你好吗？

Wǒ: Wǒ shì Xiǎo Wǔ a. Nǐ hǎo ma?

Me: I am Xiao Wu. How are you?

小亮：我很好。你呢？

Xiǎo Liàng: Wǒ hěn hǎo. Nǐ ne?

Xiao Liang: I am very good. What about you?

我：我也很好。我想今天去看电影。你能不能和我一起去看？

Wǒ: Wǒ yě hěn hǎo. Wǒ xiǎng jīntiān qù kàn diànyǐng. Nǐ néng bùnéng hé wǒ yīqǐ qù kàn?

Me: I am good. I want to go to the movies today. Would you like to go with me?

小亮：对不起。今天我和爸爸一起去医院看医生，不能去看电影了。

Xiǎo Liàng: Duìbùqǐ. Jīntiān wǒ hé bàba yīqǐ qù yīyuàn kàn yīshēng, bùnéng qù kàn diànyǐngle.

Xiao Liang: Sorry. I can't go to the movies today because I will be going to the hospital with my Dad to see a doctor.

我：那明天怎么样？

Wǒ: Nà míngtiān zěnme yàng?

Me: How about tomorrow?

小亮：明天我和妈妈去商店买东西也不能去看电影了。

Xiǎo Liàng: Míngtiān wǒ hé māmā qù shāngdiàn mǎi dōngxī yě bùnéng qù kàn diànyǐngle.

Xiao Liang: Tomorrow, my Mom and I will be going to the store to buy things, so can't go to the movies.

我：没关系。下个星期我再打个电话给你。

Wǒ: Méiguānxì. Xià gè xīngqí wǒ zài dǎ gè diànhuà gěi nǐ.

Me: It’s ok. I will call you again next week.

小亮不能去，现在我能做什么呢？谁能和我一起看电影呢？我想我还是打个电话给小喜问一问她能不能和我一起去看电影。

Xiǎo Liàng bùnéng qù, xiànzài wǒ néng zuò shénme ne? Shéi néng hé wǒ yīqǐ kàn diànyǐng ne? Wǒ xiǎng wǒ háishì dǎ gè diànhuà gěi Xiǎo Xǐ wèn yī wèn tā néng bùnéng hé wǒ yīqǐ qù kàn diànyǐng.

Xiao Liang can't go, what can I do now? Who can watch a movie with me? I think I should call Xiao Xi and ask if she can go to the movies with me.

我：喂。这是小喜吗？

Wǒ: Wèi. Zhè shì Xiǎo Xǐ ma?

Me: Hello. Is this Xiao Xi?

小喜：是啊。请问你是谁？

Xiǎo Xǐ: Shì a. Qǐngwèn nǐ shì shéi?

Xiao Xi: Yes. May I know who am I speaking to?

我：我是小五啊。你好吗？

Wǒ: Wǒ shì Xiǎo Wǔ a. Nǐ hǎo ma?

Me: I am Xiao Wu. How are you?

小喜：我很好。你呢？

Xiǎo Xǐ: Wǒ hěn hǎo. Nǐ ne?

Xiao Xi: I am very good. What about you?

我：今天你能不能和我一起去看电影？我已经打过电话给小亮，他说他今天和爸爸去医院看医生，不能和我一起去看电影。

Wǒ: Jīntiān nǐ néng bùnéng hé wǒ yīqǐ qù kàn diànyǐng? Wǒ yǐjīng dǎguò diànhuà gěi Xiǎo Liàng, tā shuō tā jīntiān hé bàba qù yīyuàn kàn yīshēng, bùnéng hé wǒ yīqǐ qù kàn diànyǐng.

Me: Can you go to the movies with me today? I have already called Xiao Liang. He said that he has to go to the hospital with his Dad to see a doctor so he can't go to the movies with me today.

小喜：对不起。我在工作，不能去看电影。

Xiǎo Xǐ: Duìbùqǐ. Wǒ zài gōngzuò, bùnéng qù kàn diànyǐng.

Xiao Xi: Sorry. I am at work, can't go to the movies.

我：什么？你在工作？

Wǒ: Shénme? Nǐ zài gōngzuò?

Me: What? You are working?

小喜：是啊。已经有一个多月了。

Xiǎo Xǐ: Shì a. Yǐjīng yǒu yīgè duō yuèle.

Xiao Xi: Yes. It has been more than a month.

我：那没关系。我们下个星期再看看怎么样？

Wǒ: Nà méiguānxì. Wǒmen xià gè xīngqí zài kàn kàn zěnme yàng?

Me: That's okay. We will see how next week?

小喜：下个星期我和小亮一起坐飞机去北京。他没说吗？

Xiǎo Xǐ: Xià gè xīngqí wǒ hé Xiǎo Liàng yīqǐ zuò fēijī qù běijīng. Tā méi shuō ma?

Xiao Xi: Next week, I will fly to Beijing with Xiao Liang. Didn't he say that?

我：没关系。再见。

Wǒ: Méiguānxì. Zàijiàn.

Me: That's okay. Goodbye.

小亮和小喜都不能和我一起去看电影。我就一个人去看电影吧。我已经有几个星期没和他们说话了。他们也没问我想不想一起去北京。我看小亮和小喜是不会再打电话给我的。

Xiǎo Liàng hé Xiǎo Xǐ dōu bùnéng hé wǒ yīqǐ qù kàn diànyǐng. Wǒ jiù yīgè rén qù kàn diànyǐng ba. Wǒ yǐjīng yǒu jǐ gè xīngqí méi hé tāmen shuōhuàle. Tāmen yě méi wèn wǒ xiǎng bùxiǎng yīqǐ qù běijīng. Wǒ kàn Xiǎo Liàng hé Xiǎo Xǐ shì bù huì zài dǎ diànhuà gěi wǒ de.

Xiao Liang and Xiao Xi can't go to the movies with me. I will go to the movies alone. I have not spoken to them for a few weeks. They didn't even ask me if I wanted to go to Beijing with them. I think Xiao Liang and Xiao Xi will not call me again.

我应该多认识几个朋友。如果有几个朋友不能和我看电影，我还有别的朋友能和我一起看电影啊。就这样吧！明天，我就出去多认识几个朋友。

Wǒ yīnggāi duō rènshì jǐ gè péngyǒu. Rúguǒ yǒu jǐ gè péngyǒu bùnéng hé wǒ kàn diànyǐng, wǒ hái yǒu bié de péngyǒu néng hé wǒ yīqǐ kàn diànyǐng a. Jiù zhèyàng ba! Míngtiān, wǒ jiù chūqù duō rènshì jǐ gè péngyǒu.

I should get to know a few more friends. If a few friends can't watch movies with me, I would still have other friends who can watch movies with me. That's right! I will go out and make more friends tomorrow.

Statistics for Story [7]

618 Total Word Count

129 Number of Unique Words

85 (56.67 %) of the 150 HSK 1 words are used in this Story

85.28 % of the Story comprise of the Extended HSK 1 words

26 New Words

New Words	Pinyin	Explanation
就	jiù	At once, right away, as soon as, then, in that case
件	jiàn	Piece (of clothe) (classifier for events, things, clothes etc)
已经	yǐjīng	Already, have
可是	kěshì	But, however
用	yòng	Use
女	nǚ	Woman, female
男	nán	Man, Male
因为	yīnwèi	Because, since, for

New Words	Pinyin	Explanation
天天	tiān tiān	Everyday
如果	rú guǒ	If, in case, in the event that
比	bǐ	Compare, contrast
到	dào	Arrive, up to (verb complement denoting completion or result of an action)
还	hái	Also, still, yet
过	guò	Over, cross, pass (time)
让	ràng	Let, allow
只	zhǐ	Only, merely, just, classifier for dogs, cats, birds and certain animals
卖	mài	Sell, sale
先	xiān	Prior, first, in advance
找	zhǎo	Find, look for, seek
走	zǒu	To walk, to go
难	nán	Difficult
话	huà	Words
所以	suǒ yǐ	Therefore, as a result, so, the reason why
出	chū	Out
要	yào	Want

New Words	Pinyin	Explanation
外国	wài guó	Foreign

[7] Buying Women's Clothes?

买女人的衣服？

我今年四十九岁，在商店里工作。商店里卖了很多衣服。那些衣服是中国来的。天气好的时候，那些衣服就卖的很好，因为有很多人来商店买东西，看见这些衣服就很喜欢，会买下来。如果天气不好，就没有人来商店买东西了，所以衣服也没人买了。

这个月天气不太好。天天只卖到几件衣服，这样下去，我就不能让女儿去大学读书了。你看，我女儿很想出国读书，可是去外国读书要用很多钱的。我看看过几天怎么样，如果还是这样的话，女儿就不能去外国的大学了。

中午的时候，有一个先生走过我的商店。他看了我的商店一下，就走到商店里面了。

我：先生，你好，你想买什么？

先生：你有没有女人的衣服？

我：在里面有很多，你想买多大的？你是不是买衣服给你的女儿？

先生：你先让我看看你有什么衣服。

看了三十分钟，那个先生看来看去，还没说他想买哪件衣服。已经下午一点了，我想去吃饭，也不能。

先生：这件衣服多少钱？

我：六十九块钱。

先生：你有大点儿的吗？

我：有。几大呢？

先生：我这么大。

我：你这么大？我去里面看看。请你坐在这个椅子上。如果你想喝茶，桌子上有杯子和茶。

先生：好，谢谢你。

他的人这么大，我哪儿去找一件这么大的女人衣服？他的女儿有男人这么大吗？我很想去吃饭，不卖了。

可是我今天一件衣服还没卖过。啊，这是什么？找到了！

我：先生，这件衣服好吗？

先生：这件衣服很好。多少钱？

我：七十九块钱。

先生：为什么这么多啊？

我：因为这件衣服很大，很难找到的。不是很多人卖，也不是很多人买。这么大也漂亮的女人衣服是很难找到的。

先生：如果我想买多点儿，六十块，好吗？

我：你想买多少件衣服？

先生：五件。

我：就卖给你七十块钱一件好吗？

先生：好吧。

我：你的女儿会很高兴的，有一个这么好的爸爸，买这么多好看的衣服给她。

先生：这些衣服不是买给她的。

我：那就是买给她的妈妈的？

先生：也不是。

我：那是买给谁的？

先生：是买给我的。我一个星期买几件这样的衣服。如果你有多点儿这样的衣服，我会天天来这儿买啊。

我：可是，这几件是女人的衣服，不是男人的衣服。

先生：是啊。我喜欢女人的衣服因为女人的衣服比男人的好看。

他给了我钱就走了。没关系了，女人，还是男人，有人买我的衣服就好了。

Pinyin and Translation [7]

我今年四十九岁，在商店里工作。商店里卖了很多衣服。那些衣服是中国来的。天气好的时候，那些衣服就卖的很好，因为有很多人来商店买东西，看见这些衣服就很喜欢，会买下来。如果天气不好，就没有人来商店买东西了，所以衣服也没人买了。

Wǒ jīnnián sìshíjiǔ suì, zài shāngdiàn lǐ gōngzuò. Shāngdiàn lǐ màile hěnduō yīfú. Nàxiē yīfú shì zhōngguó lái de. Tiānqì hǎo de shíhòu, nàxiē yīfú jiù mài de hěn hǎo, yīnwèi yǒu hěnduō rén lái shāngdiàn mǎi dōngxī, kànjiàn zhèxiē yīfú jiù hěn xǐhuān, huì mǎi xiàlái. Rúguǒ tiānqì bù hǎo, jiù méiyǒu rén lái shāngdiàn mǎi dōngxīle, suǒyǐ yīfú yě méi rén mǎile.

I am forty-nine years old and work in the store. The store sells a lot of clothes. Those clothes are from China. When the weather is good, those clothes sells very well, because there will be a lot of people visiting the store. When they see these clothes, they like them very much and will buy them. If the weather is bad, no one will come to the store to buy things, and no one will buy the clothes.

这个月天气不太好。天天只卖到几件衣服，这样下去，我就不能让女儿去大学读书了。你看，我女儿很想出国读书，可是去外国读书要用很多钱的。我看看过几天怎么样，如果还是这样的话，女儿就不能去外国的大学了。

Zhège yuè tiānqì bù tài hǎo. Tiāntiān zhǐ mài dào jǐ jiàn yīfú, zhèyàng xiàqù, wǒ jiù bùnéng ràng nǚ'ér qù dàxué dúshūle. Nǐ kàn, wǒ nǚ'ér hěn xiǎng chūguó dúshū, kěshì qù wàiguó dúshū yào yòng hěnduō qián de. Wǒ kàn kànguò jǐ tiān zěnme yàng, rúguǒ háishì zhèyàng dehuà, nǚ'ér jiù bùnéng qù wàiguó de dàxuéle.

The weather has not been very good this month. I have only sold a few clothes each day, so I won't be able to let my daughter go to university. You see, my daughter wants to go abroad to study, but it costs a lot of money to study abroad. I will see how it goes for the next few days. If this continues, my daughter cannot go to an overseas university to study.

中午的时候，有一个先生走过我的商店。他看了我的商店一下，就走到商店里面了。

Zhōngwǔ de shíhòu, yǒu yīgè xiānshēng zǒuguò wǒ de shāngdiàn. Tā kànle wǒ de shāngdiàn yīxià, jiù zǒu dào shāngdiàn lǐmiànle.

At noon, a gentleman walked passed my store. He took a look at my store and then went in.

我：先生，你好，你想买什么？

Wǒ: Xiānshēng, nǐ hǎo, nǐ xiǎng mǎi shénme?

Me: Hello, sir. What would you like to buy?

先生：你有没有女人的衣服？

Xiānshēng: Nǐ yǒu méiyǒu nǚrén de yīfú?

Sir: Do you have any women's clothes?

我：在里面有很多，你想买多大的？你是不是买衣服给你的女儿？

Wǒ: Zài lǐmiàn yǒu hěnduō, nǐ xiǎng mǎi duōdà de? Nǐ shì bùshì mǎi yīfú gěi nǐ de nǚ'ér?

Me: There are a lot inside, what size do you want? Are you buying for your daughter?

先生：你先让我看看你有什么衣服。

Xiānshēng: Nǐ xiān ràng wǒ kàn kàn nǐ yǒu shé me yīfú.

Sir: Let me have a look first.

看了三十分钟，那个先生看来看去，还没说他想买哪件衣服。已经下午一点了，我想去吃饭，也不能。

Kànle sānshí fēnzhōng, nàgè xiānshēng kàn lái kàn qù, hái méi shuō tā xiǎng mǎi nǎ jiàn yīfú. Yǐjīng xiàwǔ yīdiǎnle, wǒ xiǎng qù chīfàn, yě bùnéng.

After thirty minutes, the gentleman still hasn't said which clothes he wanted to buy. It's already so late in the afternoon, I want to go for lunch.

先生：这件衣服多少钱？

Xiānshēng: Zhè jiàn yīfú duōshǎo qián?

Sir: How much is this dress?

我：六十九块钱。

Wǒ: Liùshíjiǔ kuài qián.

Me: Sixty-nine dollars.

先生：你有大点儿的吗？

Xiānshēng: Nǐ yǒu dà diǎn er de ma?

Sir: Do you have a bigger one?

我：有。几大呢？

Wǒ: Yǒu. Jǐ dà ne?

Me: Yes. How big do you want?

先生：我这么大。

Xiānshēng: Wǒ zhème dà.

Sir: My size.

我：你这么大？我去里面看看。请你坐在这个椅子上。如果你想喝茶，桌子上有杯子和茶。

Wǒ: Nǐ zhème dà? Wǒ qù lǐmiàn kàn kàn. Qǐng nǐ zuò zài zhège yǐzi shàng. Rúguǒ nǐ xiǎng hē chá, zhuōzi shàng yǒu bēizi hé chá.

Me: Your size? I will go inside and have a look. Please have a seat. If you want to drink tea, there are cups and tea on the table.

先生：好，谢谢你。

Xiānshēng: Hǎo, xièxiè nǐ.

Sir: Ok, thank you.

他的人这么大，我哪儿去找一件这么大的女人衣服？他的女儿有男人这么大吗？我很想去吃饭，不卖了。

可是我今天一件衣服还没卖过。啊，这是什么？找到了！

Tā de rén zhème dà, wǒ nǎ'er qù zhǎo yī jiàn zhème dà de nǚrén yīfú? Tā de nǚ'ér yǒu nánrén zhème dà ma? Wǒ hěn xiǎng qù chīfàn, bù màile. Kěshì wǒ jīntiān yī jiàn yīfú hái méi màiguò. A, zhè shì shénme? Zhǎodàole!

He is so big, where can I find such a large woman's clothes? Is his daughter as big as a man? I really want to go for lunch and not sell to this man. But I have not sold a single piece of clothing today. Ah, what is this? Found it!

我：先生，这件衣服好吗？

Wǒ: Xiānshēng, zhè jiàn yīfú hǎo ma?

Me: Sir, is this dress ok?

先生：这件衣服很好。多少钱？

Xiānshēng: Zhè jiàn yīfú hěn hǎo. Duōshǎo qián?

Sir: This dress is very good. How much is it?

我：七十九块钱。

Wǒ: Qīshíjiǔ kuài qián.

Me: Seventy-nine dollars.

先生：为什么这么多啊？

Xiānshēng: Wèishéme zhème duō a?

Sir: Why is it so much?

我：因为这件衣服很大，很难找到的。不是很多人卖，也不是很多人买。这么大也漂亮的女人衣服是很难找到的。

Wǒ: Yīnwèi zhè jiàn yīfú hěn dà, hěn nán zhǎodào de. Bùshì hěnduō rén mài, yě bùshì hěnduō rén mǎi. Zhème dà yě piàoliang de nǚrén yīfú shì hěn nán zhǎodào de.

Me: Because this kind of big dress is very hard to find. Not many people will sell, and not many people will buy. Such a large and beautiful dress is very hard to find.

先生：如果我想买多点儿，六十块，好吗？

Xiānshēng: Rúguǒ wǒ xiǎng mǎi duō diǎn er, liùshí kuài, hǎo ma?

Sir: If I buy more, sixty dollars, okay?

我：你想买多少件衣服？

Wǒ: Nǐ xiǎng mǎi duōshǎo jiàn yīfú?

Me: How many do you want to buy?

先生：五件。

Xiānshēng: Wǔ jiàn.

Sir: Five pieces.

我：就卖给你七十块钱一件好吗？

Wǒ: Jiù mài gěi nǐ qīshí kuài qián yī jiàn hǎo ma?

Me: I will sell to you for seventy dollars, ok?

先生：好吧。

Xiānshēng: Hǎo ba.

Sir: Ok.

我：你的女儿会很高兴的，有一个这么好的爸爸，买这么多好看的衣服给她。

Wǒ: Nǐ de nǚ'ér huì hěn gāoxìng de, yǒu yīgè zhème hǎo de bàba, mǎi zhème duō hǎokàn de yīfú gěi tā.

Me: Your daughter will be very happy because she has such a good father who buys so many beautiful dresses for her.

先生：这些衣服不是买给她的。

Xiānshēng: Zhèxiē yīfú bùshì mǎi gěi tā de.

Sir: These dresses are not for her.

我：那就是买给她的妈妈的？

Wǒ: Nà jiùshì mǎi gěi tā de māmā de?

Me: Then are these for her mother?

先生：也不是。

Xiānshēng: Yě bùshì.

Sir: No they are not.

我：那是买给谁的？

Wǒ: Nà shì mǎi gěi shéi de?

Me: Then, who are they for?

先生：是买给我的。我一个星期买几件这样的衣服。如果你有多点儿这样的衣服，我会天天来这儿买啊。

Xiānshēng: Shì mǎi gěi wǒ de. Wǒ yīgè xīngqí mǎi jǐ jiàn zhèyàng de yīfú. Rúguǒ nǐ yǒu duō diǎn er zhèyàng de yīfú, wǒ huì tiāntiān lái zhè'er mǎi a.

Sir: I am buying them for myself. I will buy a few of these dresses every week. If you have more dresses like this, I will come and buy from you every day.

我：可是，这几件是女人的衣服，不是男人的衣服。

Wǒ: Kěshì, zhè jǐ jiàn shì nǚrén de yīfú, bùshì nánrén de yīfú.

Me: But these are women's clothes, not men's clothes.

先生：是啊。我喜欢女人的衣服因为女人的衣服比男人的好看。

Xiānshēng: Shì a. Wǒ xǐhuān nǚrén de yīfú yīnwèi nǚrén de yīfú bǐ nánrén de hǎokàn.

Sir: Yes. I like women's clothes because women's clothes look better than men's.

他给了我钱就走了。没关系了，女人，还是男人，有人买我的衣服就好了。

Tā gěile wǒ qián jiù zǒule. Méiguānxìle, nǚrén, háishì nánrén, yǒurén mǎi wǒ de yīfú jiù hǎole.

He paid me and left. It doesn't matter, woman, or man, as long as someone buys my clothes.

Statistics for Story [8]

649 Total Word Count

140 Number of Unique Words

94 (62.67 %) of the 150 HSK 1 words are used in this Story

87.21 % of the Story comprise of the Extended HSK 1 words

28 New Words

New Words	Pinyin	Explanation
玛丽	mǎ lì	Mary
就	jiù	At once, right away, as soon as, then, in that case
件	jiàn	Piece (of clothe) (classifier for events, things, clothes etc)
已经	yǐjīng	Already, have
用	yòng	Use
女	nǚ	Woman, female
天天	tiān tiān	Everyday
如果	rú guǒ	If, in case, in the event that

New Words	Pinyin	Explanation
到	dào	Arrive, up to (verb complement denoting completion or result of an action)
过	guò	Over, cross, pass (time)
只	zhǐ	Only, merely, just, classifier for dogs, cats, birds and certain animals
找	zhǎo	Find, look for, seek
出	chū	Out
外国	wài guó	Foreign
外人	wài rén	Outsiders
放	fàng	Put, place
快	kuài	Fast, quickly, soon
要	yào	Want
时间	shíjiān	Time
见	jiàn	See, meet
为什么	wèishéme	Why
才	cái	Only
把	bǎ	to handle
门	mén	Door
起来	qǐlái	to stand up, to get up
再	zài	Again

New Words	Pinyin	Explanation
听说	tīng shuō	Heard
先	xiān	Prior, first, in advance

[8] Our Son's Girlfriend

儿子的女朋友

爸爸：今天几号？

妈妈：今天是五月四号。为什么？

爸爸：儿子下个星期五就回到家了。

妈妈：你是不是很高兴？

爸爸：我是很高兴儿子回家。你不高兴吗？

妈妈：我也很高兴儿子回来。他已经住在美国三年了。他的飞机几点到啊？

爸爸：我想是中午吧。

妈妈：我想给儿子打个电话问一问。

爸爸：美国现在是上午六点。我看他已经起来了。

妈妈：喂。儿子。是妈妈。

儿子：喂。妈妈，我好想你啊。

妈妈：我和爸爸也好想你啊。你下个星期回来，飞机几点到这儿？

儿子：下午五点到。你们不用来了。我打出租车回家。

妈妈：好吧。下个星期见。

儿子：妈妈，对不起，我在医院里工作，没有时间打电话给你们。我会在家里住一个月。到时候，我天天都见到你们了。

到了下个星期五：

爸爸：现在六点了。我想，儿子就快到家了。你把桌子和椅子上的东西放好了没有？儿子不喜欢在他的桌子和椅子放这么多东西的。

妈妈：已经放好了。你这件衣服不好看。

爸爸：没关系，我们只是看儿子，也不是什么外人。车到了。快出去。

车门打开的时候，下车的不是儿子，是一个外国的女人。在她的后面是我们的儿子。

儿子：爸爸，妈妈，看到你们太好了。

爸爸：这小姐是谁啊？

儿子：她是我的女朋友。她的名字是玛丽。我们先去里面再说。

儿子和玛丽放好他们的东西后，就坐在椅子上和我们一起喝茶。

妈妈：你什么时候认识玛丽啊？

儿子：已经有三个月了。她是美国人，在我医院工作的。

爸爸：他会不会说汉语？

儿子：她会说一点儿汉语。

玛丽：爸爸妈妈，你们好。

妈妈：这么快就叫我们爸爸妈妈了。

儿子：妈妈，她说的不好，你不要不高兴，好吗？

爸爸：你妈妈是说不要她叫我们爸爸妈妈。我们现在才认识她。你也没有说过你有一个外国的女朋友。

妈妈：她在中国有没有朋友？她在中国住哪儿？

儿子：她会住在这儿。

妈妈：好吧，你们坐一下。我去做菜。玛丽吃不吃中国菜？如果她不吃，我们就去饭馆吃吧。

玛丽：我很喜欢吃中国菜。我听说你做的中国菜很好吃。

妈妈：好了。你坐一下。

爸爸：我去看你妈妈做什么菜。你们坐一下。

玛丽：好。谢谢爸爸妈妈。

爸爸：不客气。

我们在里面做菜的时候：

妈妈：你看那个玛丽怎么样？

爸爸：我们才认识她。我们多给她点儿时间吧。怎么了？你不喜欢她？

妈妈：她是个外国人啊。中国有这么多好的女人，为什么儿子去找个外国女人做女朋友呢？

爸爸：你不要这么快就想到她是不好的。他们会在这儿住一个月，我们有很多时间和他们在一起。我们先看看怎么样，好吗？

妈妈：好吧。

过了一个月，我们认识玛丽后，就很喜欢她，说儿子找到了一个很好的女朋友。

Pinyin and Translation [8]

爸爸：今天几号？

Bàba: Jīntiān jǐ hào?

Dad: What is the date today?

妈妈：今天是五月四号。为什么？

Māmā: Jīntiān shì wǔ yuè sì hào. Wèishéme?

Mom: Today is May 4th. Why?

爸爸：儿子下个星期五就回到家了。

Bàba: Érzi xià gè xīngqíwǔ jiù huí dàojiāle.

Dad: Our son will be home next Friday.

妈妈：你是不是很高兴？

Māmā: Nǐ shì bùshì hěn gāoxìng?

Mom: Are you happy?

爸爸：我是很高兴儿子回家。你不高兴吗？

Bàba: Wǒ shì hěn gāoxìng ér zǐ huí jiā. Nǐ bù gāoxìng ma?

Dad: I am very happy that our son is coming home. Are you not happy?

妈妈：我也很高兴儿子回来。他已经住在美国三年了。他的飞机几点到啊?

Māmā: Wǒ yě hěn gāoxìng ér zǐ huílái. Tā yǐjīng zhù zài měiguó sān niánle. Tā de fēijī jǐ diǎn dào a?

Mom: I am also very happy that our son will be back. He has been living in the United States for three years. When is his plane arriving?

爸爸：我想是中午吧。

Bàba: Wǒ xiǎng shì zhōngwǔ ba.

Dad: I think it will be at noon.

妈妈：我想给儿子打个电话问一问。

Māmā: Wǒ xiǎng gěi érzi dǎ gè diànhuà wèn yī wèn.

Mom: I want to call our son and ask.

爸爸：美国现在是上午六点。我看他已经起来了。

Bàba: Měiguó xiànzài shì shàngwǔ liù diǎn. Wǒ kàn tā yǐjīng qǐláile.

Dad: It is now six in the morning in the United States . I think he will be up.

妈妈：喂。儿子。是妈妈。

Māmā: Wèi. Érzi. Shì māmā.

Mom: Hello. Son. This is Mom.

儿子：喂。妈妈，我好想你啊。

Érzi: Wèi. Māmā, wǒ hǎo xiǎng nǐ a.

Son: Hello. Mom, I miss you so much.

妈妈：我和爸爸也好想你啊。你下个星期回来，飞机几点到这儿？

Māmā: Wǒ hé bàba yě hǎo xiǎng nǐ a. Nǐ xià gè xīngqí huílái, fēijī jǐ diǎn dào zhè'er?

Mom: Your Dad and I miss you too. What time does your plane arrive next week?

儿子：下午五点到。你们不用来了。我打出租车回家。

Érzi: Xiàwǔ wǔ diǎn dào. Nǐmen bùyòng láile. Wǒ dǎ chūzū chē huí jiā.

Son: At five o'clock in the afternoon. You don't have to come. I am taking a taxi home.

妈妈：好吧。下个星期见。

Māmā: Hǎo ba. Xià gè xīngqí jiàn.

Mom: Ok. See you next week.

儿子：妈妈，对不起，我在医院里工作，没有时间打电话给你们。我会在家里住一个月。到时候，我天天都见到你们了。

Érzi: Māmā, duìbùqǐ, wǒ zài yīyuàn lǐ gōngzuò, méiyǒu shíjiān dǎ diànhuà gěi nǐmen. Wǒ huì zài jiālǐ zhù yīgè yuè. Dào shíhòu, wǒ tiāntiān dōu jiàn dào nǐmenle.

Son: Mom, I am sorry, I work in the hospital and have no time to call you. I will stay at home for a month and I will be seeing you every day.

到了下个星期五：

Dàole xià gè xīngqíwǔ:

Next Friday:

爸爸：现在六点了。我想，儿子就快到家了。你把桌子和椅子上的东西放好了没有？儿子不喜欢在他的桌子和椅子放这么多东西的。

Bàba: Xiànzài liù diǎnle. Wǒ xiǎng, érzi jiù kuài dàojiāle. Nǐ bǎ zhuōzi hé yǐzi shàng de dōngxī fàng hǎole méiyǒu? Érzi bù xǐhuān zài tā de zhuōzi hé yǐzi fàng zhème duō dōngxī de.

Dad: It's six o'clock now. I think our son will be home soon. Have you kept the things on the table and chair? Our son doesn't like to have so many things on his desk and chair.

妈妈：已经放好了。你这件衣服不好看。

Māmā: Yǐjīng fàng hǎole. Nǐ zhè jiàn yīfú bù hǎokàn.

Mom: They have already been put away. Your shirt doesn't look good.

爸爸：没关系，我们只是看儿子，也不是什么外人。车到了。快出去。

Bàba: Méiguānxì, wǒmen zhǐshì kàn érzi, yě bùshì shénme wàirén. Chē dàole. Kuài chūqù.

Dad: It doesn't matter. It is just our son, not any outsiders. The car is here. Let's go out.

车门打开的时候，下车的不是儿子，是一个外国的女人。在她的后面是我们的儿子。

Chēmén dǎkāi de shíhòu, xià chē de bùshì érzi, shì yīgè wàiguó de nǚrén. Zài tā de hòumiàn shì wǒmen de érzi.

When the car door was opened, it wasnt our son who got off the car. It was a foreign woman. Behind her was our son.

儿子：爸爸，妈妈，看到你们太好了。

Érzi: Bàba, māmā, kàn dào nǐmen tài hǎole.

Son: Dad, Mom, it's great to see you.

爸爸：这小姐是谁啊？

Bàba: Zhè xiǎojiě shì shéi a?

Dad: Who is this lady?

儿子：她是我的女朋友。她的名字是玛丽。我们先去里面再说。

Érzi: Tā shì wǒ de nǚ péngyǒu. Tā de míngzì shì Mǎlì. Wǒmen xiān qù lǐmiàn zàishuō.

Son: She is my girlfriend. Her name is Mary. Let's go inside and talk.

儿子和玛丽放好他们的东西后，就坐在椅子上和我们一起喝茶。

Érzi hé mǎlì fàng hǎo tāmen de dōngxī hòu, jiùzuò zài yǐzi shàng hé wǒmen yīqǐ hē chá.

After our son and Mary put their things, they sat down and had tea with us.

妈妈：你什么时候认识玛丽啊？

Māmā: Nǐ shénme shíhòu rènshì mǎlì a?

Mom: When did you meet Mary?

儿子：已经有三个月了。她是美国人，在我医院工作的。

Érzi: Yǐjīng yǒusān gè yuèle. Tā shì měiguó rén, zài wǒ yīyuàn gōngzuò de.

Son: It has been three months. She is an American and works at my hospital.

爸爸：她会不会说汉语？

Bàba: Tā huì bù huì shuō hànyǔ?

Dad: Can she speak Chinese?

儿子：她会说一点儿汉语。

Érzi: Tā huì shuō yīdiǎn er hànyǔ.

Son: She can speak a little Chinese.

玛丽：爸爸妈妈，你们好。

Mǎlì: Bàba māmā, nǐmen hǎo.

Mary: Mom and Dad, how are you.

妈妈：这么快就叫我们爸爸妈妈了。

Māmā: Zhème kuài jiù jiào wǒmen bàba māmāle.

Mom: She is calling us mom and dad so soon.

儿子：妈妈，她说的不好，你不要不高兴，好吗？

Érzi: Māmā, tā shuō de bù hǎo, nǐ bùyào bù gāoxìng, hǎo ma?

Son: Mom, if she doesn't speak well, please don't be upset, okay?

爸爸：你妈妈是说不要她叫我们爸爸妈妈。我们现在才认识她。你也没有说过你有一个外国的女朋友。

Bàba: Nǐ māmā shì shuō bu yào tā jiào wǒmen bàba māmā. Wǒmen xiànzài cái rènshì tā. Nǐ yě méiyǒu shuōguò nǐ yǒu yīgè wàiguó de nǚ péngyǒu.

Dad: What your Mom saying is she should not call us Mom and Dad. We just got to know her. You have never said that you have a foreign girlfriend.

妈妈：她在中国有没有朋友？她在中国住哪儿？

Māmā: Tā zài zhōngguó yǒu méiyǒu péngyǒu? Tā zài zhōngguó zhù nǎ'er?

Mom: Does she have any friends in China? Where is she going to stay in China?

儿子：她会住在这儿。

Érzi: Tā huì zhù zài zhè'er.

Son: She will be staying here.

妈妈：好吧，你们坐一下。我去做菜。玛丽吃不吃中国菜？如果她不吃，我们就去饭馆吃吧。

Māmā: Hǎo ba, nǐmen zuò yīxià. Wǒ qù zuò cài. Mǎlì chī bù chī zhōngguó cài? Rúguǒ tā bù chī, wǒmen jiù qù fànguǎn chī ba.

Mom: Ok, both of you sit here for a while. I am going to cook. Does Mary eat Chinese food? If she doesn't eat, we should go to the restaurant to eat.

玛丽：我很喜欢吃中国菜。我听说你做的中国菜很好吃。

Mǎlì: Wǒ hěn xǐhuān chī zhōngguó cài. Wǒ tīng shuō nǐ zuò de zhōngguó cài hěn hào chī.

Mary: I like Chinese food very much. I heard that you cook very delicious Chinese dishes.

妈妈：好了。你坐一下。

Māmā: Hǎole. Nǐ zuò yīxià.

Mom: Ok. Please sit for a while.

爸爸：我去看你妈妈做什么菜。你们坐一下。

Bàba: Wǒ qù kàn nǐ māmā zuò shénme cài. Nǐmen zuò yīxià

Dad: I am going to see what is your Mom cooking. You sit for a while.

玛丽：好。谢谢爸爸妈妈。

Mǎlì: Hǎo. Xièxiè bàba māmā.

Mary: Ok. Thank you, Mom and Dad.

爸爸：不客气。

Bàba: Bù kèqì.

Dad: You are welcome.

我们在里面做菜的时候：

Wǒmen zài lǐmiàn zuò cài de shíhòu:

When we are cooking:

妈妈：你看那个玛丽怎么样？

Māmā: Nǐ kàn nàgè mǎlì zěnme yàng?

Mom: What do you think of that Mary?

爸爸：我们才认识她。我们多给她点儿时间吧。怎么了？你不喜欢她？

Bàba: Wǒmen cái rènshì tā. Wǒmen duō gěi tā diǎn er shíjiān ba. Zěnmeliǎo? Nǐ bù xǐhuān tā?

Dad: We just got to know her. Let's give her more time. Why? You don't like her?

妈妈：她是个外国人啊。中国有这么多好的女人，为什么儿子去找个外国女人做女朋友呢？

Māmā: Tā shìgè wàiguó rén a. Zhōngguó yǒu zhème duō hǎo de nǚrén, wèishéme érzi qù zhǎo gè wàiguó nǚrén zuò nǚ péngyǒu ne?

Mom: She is a foreigner. There are so many good women in China, why does our son have to look for a foreign woman to be his girlfriend?

爸爸：你不要这么快就想到她是不好的。他们会在这儿住一个月，我们有很多时间和他们在一起。我们先看看怎么样，好吗？

Bàba: Nǐ bùyào zhème kuài jiù xiǎngdào tā shì bù hǎo de. Tāmen huì zài zhè'er zhù yīgè yuè, wǒmen yǒu hěnduō shíjiān hé tāmen zài yīqǐ. Wǒmen xiān kàn kàn zěnme yàng, hǎo ma?

Dad: Please don't think that she is so bad. They will be staying here for a month and we will have a lot of time with them. Let's see what happens first, ok?

妈妈：好吧。

Māmā: Hǎo ba.

Mom: Ok.

过了一个月，我们认识玛丽后，就很喜欢她，说儿子找到了一个很好的女朋友。

Guòle yīgè yuè, wǒmen rènshì mǎlì hòu, jiù hěn xǐhuān tā, shuō érzi zhǎodàole yīgè hěn hǎo de nǚ péngyǒu.

After we got to know Mary for a month, we like her very much and said that our son had found a good girlfriend.

Statistics for Story [9]

637 Total Word Count

121 Number of Unique Words

75 (50.0 %) of the 150 HSK 1 words are used in this Story

80.69 % of the Story comprise of the Extended HSK 1 words

26 New Words

New Words	Pinyin	Explanation
小亮	Xiǎo Liàng	Name of a person
小喜	Xiǎo Xǐ	Name of a person
小五	Xiǎo Wǔ	Name of a person
就	jiù	At once, right away, as soon as, then, in that case
天天	tiān tiān	Everyday
如果	rú guǒ	If, in case, in the event that
还	hái	Also, still, yet
过	guò	Over, cross, pass (time)
只	zhǐ	Only, merely, just,

New Words	Pinyin	Explanation
		classifier for dogs, cats, birds and certain animals
要	yào	Want
放	fàng	Put, place
把	bǎ	to handle
难	nán	Difficult
到	dào	Arrive, up to (verb complement denoting completion or result of an action)
快	kuài	Fast, quickly, soon
卖	mài	Sell, sale
比	bǐ	Compare, contrast
为什么	wèishéme	Why
话	huà	Words
因为	yīnwèi	Because, since, for
让	ràng	Let, allow
对	duì	To, towards
可以	kěyǐ	Can
用	yòng	Use
可是	kěshì	But, however
泡茶	pào chá	Make tea

[9] Cook and Make Tea

泡茶和做菜

小亮：我想学习怎么样喝茶。

小喜：学习喝茶？喝茶有什么好学习的?

小亮：我想学什么茶是好喝，什么茶是不好的。

小喜：买茶的时候，问那个卖茶的人吧。

小亮：不是这样的。茶不能太热也不能太冷喝的。很难问卖茶的人。我想买几本喝茶的书来学习。

小喜：我看你是想多了。喝茶不就是这样喝的吗？

小亮：不是的。你把你的茶放在哪儿？

小喜：我把茶放在电视的后面。

小亮：不能把茶放在那儿的。电视太热了，茶放在那儿会不好喝的。

小喜：谁说的？我的茶很好喝。你来一点儿吧。你的杯子在哪儿？

小亮：在这儿。让我喝一喝你杯茶。

小喜：怎么样？好喝吗？

小亮：你要不要喝我的茶？看谁的茶好喝？

小喜：好啊。你的茶比我的茶好喝的多了。为什么呢？

小亮：我看这本喝茶的书学习泡茶。我在这本书上学习泡茶的。

小喜：你说的对啊，我不能把茶放在电视的后面。我就把茶放在前面吧。

小亮：什么？你也不能放茶在电视前面，还是太热了。

小喜：那我放茶在桌子上，好不好？

小亮：还有，泡茶要用很热的水，如果不热的话，茶就不好喝了。

小喜：那你有没有学怎么做菜呢？

小亮：我没有学习做菜，因为我很少做菜。你呢？

小喜：我想学怎么做中国菜。

小亮：你在哪儿学啊?

小喜：在书里面学的。

小亮：看书学习做中国菜，会不会很难？

小喜：不会很难的。只要你喜欢，就不难学习做菜。

小亮：小五在哪儿？他在做什么？

小喜：你要不要打个电话给他？

小亮：还是你打电话给他吧。我还要去里面泡茶。

小喜：喂，是不是小五啊？

小五：是。请问你是谁？

小喜：我是小喜。小五，你好。你在做什么？要不要过来我的家？小亮也在这儿。

小五：好啊。我这就过去。可是，我下午四点想去医院看医生。你们那儿可以打出租车吗？

小喜：这儿有很多出租车。

小五：好。我现在就去你的家。

小五到了小喜的家：

小五：你们在做什么呢？

小亮：我在泡茶给你们喝。

小喜：我在做中国菜给你们吃。

小五：太好了。我想喝茶也想吃中国菜。几时能喝到茶和吃到饭菜呢？

小亮：我的茶快要好了。你坐一下吧。

小喜：我的菜也快要做好了。

小五：太好了。我一来就有茶喝，有菜吃了。

小喜：好吃吗？

小五：很好吃啊。比我昨天在饭馆吃的好多了。

小亮：茶好喝吗？

小五：很好喝。这是什么茶？

小亮：是中国茶。

小五：茶和菜都这么好，你们快点儿一起去开饭馆吧。我会天天去你们的饭馆喝茶，吃饭的。

Pinyin and Translation [9]

小亮：我想学习怎么样喝茶。

Xiǎo Liàng: Wǒ xiǎng xuéxí zěnme yàng hē chá.

Xiao Liang: I want to learn how to drink tea.

小喜：学习喝茶？喝茶有什么好学习的?

Xiǎo Xǐ: Xuéxí hē chá? Hē chá yǒu shé me hào xuéxí de?

Xiao Xi: Learn how to drink tea? What is there to learn about drinking tea?

小亮：我想学什么茶是好喝，什么茶是不好的。

Xiǎo Liàng: Wǒ xiǎng xué shénme chá shì hǎo hē, shénme chá shì bù hǎo de.

Xiao Liang: I want to learn which tea is good, which tea is not good.

小喜：买茶的时候，问那个卖茶的人吧。

Xiǎo Xǐ: Mǎi chá de shíhòu, wèn nàgè mài chá de rén ba.

Xiao Xi: When you are buying tea, just ask the person who sells tea.

小亮：不是这样的。茶不能太热也不能太冷喝的。很难问卖茶的人。我想买几本喝茶的书来学习。

Xiǎo Liàng: Bùshì zhèyàng de. Chá bùnéng tài rè yě bùnéng tài lěng hē de. Hěn nán wèn mài chá de rén. Wǒ xiǎng mǎi jǐ běn hē chá de shū lái xuéxí.

Xiao Liang: This is not the case. Tea can't be too hot or too cold. It is difficult to ask the person who sells tea. I want to buy a few books to learn.

小喜：我看你是想多了。喝茶不就是这样喝的吗？

Xiǎo Xǐ: Wǒ kàn nǐ shì xiǎng duōle. Hē chá bù jiùshì zhèyàng hē de ma?

Xiao Xi: I think you are thinking too much. Isn't drinking tea like this?

小亮：不是的。你把你的茶放在哪儿？

Xiǎo Liàng: Bùshì de. Nǐ bǎ nǐ de chá fàng zài nǎ'er?

Xiao Liang: No. Where do you put your tea leaves?

小喜：我把茶放在电视的后面。

Xiǎo Xǐ: Wǒ bǎ chá fàng zài diànshì de hòumiàn.

Xiao Xi: I put the tea leaves behind the TV.

小亮：不能把茶放在那儿的。电视太热了，茶放在那儿会不好喝的。

Xiǎo Liàng: Bùnéng bǎ chá fàng zài nà'er de. Diànshì tài rèle, chá fàng zài nà'er huì bù hǎo hē de.

Xiao Liang: You can't put tea leaves there. The TV is too hot, and the tea will not be good to drink.

小喜：谁说的？我的茶很好喝。你来一点儿吧。你的杯子在哪儿？

Xiǎo Xǐ: Shéi shuō de? Wǒ de chá hěn hǎo hē. Nǐ lái yīdiǎn er ba. Nǐ de bēizi zài nǎ'er?

Xiao Xi: Who say? My tea is very good. Come, have some. Where is your cup?

小亮：在这儿。让我喝一喝你杯茶。

Xiǎo Liàng: Zài zhè'er. Ràng wǒ hè yīhē nǐ bēi chá.

Xiao Liang: Here. Let me drink your cup of tea.

小喜：怎么样？好喝吗？

Xiǎo Xǐ: Zěnme yàng? Hǎo hē ma?

Xiao Xi: How is it?

小亮：你要不要喝我的茶？看谁的茶好喝？

Xiǎo Liàng: Nǐ yào bùyào hē wǒ de chá? Kàn shéi de chá hǎo hē?

Xiao Liang: Do you want to drink my tea? Let's see whose tea is better?

小喜：好啊。你的茶比我的茶好喝的多了。为什么呢？

Xiǎo Xǐ: Hǎo a. Nǐ de chá bǐ wǒ de chá hǎo hē de duōle. Wèishéme ne?

Xiao Xi: Your tea taste much better than mine. Why is that?

小亮：我看这本喝茶的书学习泡茶。我在这本书上学习泡茶的。

Xiǎo Liàng: Wǒ kàn zhè běn hē chá de shū xuéxí pào chá. Wǒ zài zhè běn shū shàng xuéxí pào chá de.

Xiao Liang: I am reading this book on how to make tea. I learnt how to make tea from this book.

小喜：你说的对啊，我不能把茶放在电视的后面。我就把茶放在前面吧。

Xiǎo Xǐ: Nǐ shuō de duì a, wǒ bùnéng bǎ chá fàng zài diànshì de hòumiàn. Wǒ jiù bǎ chá fàng zài qiánmiàn ba.

Xiao Xi: You are right, I can't put the tea leaves behind the TV. I will put the tea leaves in front.

小亮：什么？你也不能放茶在电视前面，还是太热了。

Xiǎo Liàng: Shénme? Nǐ yě bùnéng fàng chá zài diànshì qiánmiàn, háishì tài rèle.

Xiao Liang: What? You can't put the tea leaves in front of the TV, it's still too hot.

小喜：那我放茶在桌子上，好不好？

Xiǎo Xǐ: Nà wǒ fàng chá zài zhuōzi shàng, hǎobù hǎo?

Xiao Xi: Then I put the tea leaves on the table, ok?

小亮：还有，泡茶要用很热的水，如果不热的话，茶就不好喝了。

Xiǎo Liàng: Hái yǒu, pào chá yào yòng hěn rè de shuǐ, rúguǒ bù rè dehuà, chá jiù bù hǎo hēle.

Xiao Liang: Also, brewing tea requires very hot water. If it is not hot enough, the tea will not be nice to drink.

小喜：那你有没有学怎么做菜呢？

Xiǎo Xǐ: Nà nǐ yǒu méiyǒu xué zěnme zuò cài ne?

Xiao Xi: Then, do you learn how to cook?

小亮：我没有学习做菜，因为我很少做菜。你呢？

Xiǎo Liàng: Wǒ méiyǒu xuéxí zuò cài, yīnwèi wǒ hěn shǎo zuò cài. Nǐ ne?

Xiao Liang: I didn't learn how to cook because I rarely cook. What about you?

小喜：我想学怎么做中国菜。

Xiǎo Xǐ: Wǒ xiǎng xué zěnme zuò zhōngguó cài.

Xiao Xi: I want to learn how to cook Chinese food.

小亮：你在哪儿学啊?

Xiǎo Liàng: Nǐ zài nǎ'er xué a?

Xiao Liang: Where do you learn from?

小喜：在书里面学的。

Xiǎo Xǐ: Zài shū lǐmiàn xué de.

Xiao Xi: Learnt from books.

小亮：看书学习做中国菜，会不会很难？

Xiǎo Liàng: Kànshū xuéxí zuò zhōngguó cài, huì bù huì hěn nán?

Xiao Liang: Is it hard to learn how to cook Chinese food from books?

小喜：不会很难的。只要你喜欢，就不难学习做菜。

Xiǎo Xǐ: Bù huì hěn nán de. Zhǐyào nǐ xǐhuān, jiù bù nán xuéxí zuò cài.

Xiao Xi: It won't be difficult. As long as you like it, it is not difficult to learn how to cook.

小亮：小五在哪儿？他在做什么？

Xiǎo Liàng: Xiǎo wǔ zài nǎ'er? Tā zài zuò shénme?

Xiao Liang: Where is Xiao Wu? What is he doing?

小喜：你要不要打个电话给他？

Xiǎo Xǐ: Nǐ yào bùyào dǎ gè diànhuà gěi tā?

Xiao Xi: Do you want to call him?

小亮：还是你打电话给他吧。我还要去里面泡茶。

Xiǎo Liàng: Háishì nǐ dǎ diànhuà gěi tā ba. Wǒ hái yào qù lǐmiàn pào chá.

Xiao Liang: I think you should call him. I have to go in and make tea.

小喜：喂，是不是小五啊？

Xiǎo Xǐ: Wèi, shì bùshì Xiǎo Wǔ a?

Xiao Xi: Hey, is this Xiao Wu?

小五：是。请问你是谁？

Xiǎo Wǔ: Shì. Qǐngwèn nǐ shì shéi?

Xiao Wu: Yes. May I know who is this?

小喜：我是小喜。小五，你好。你在做什么？要不要过来我的家？小亮也在这儿。

Xiǎo Xǐ: Wǒ shì Xiǎo Xǐ. Xiǎo Wǔ, nǐ hǎo. Nǐ zài zuò shénme? Yào bùyào guòlái wǒ de jiā? Xiǎo Liàng yě zài zhè'er.

Xiao Xi: I am Xiao Xi. Xiao Wu, how are you? What are you doing? Do you want to come to my house? Xiao Liang is here too.

小五：好啊。我这就过去。可是，我下午四点想去医院看医生。你们那儿可以打出租车吗？

Xiǎo Wǔ: Hǎo a. Wǒ zhè jiù guòqù. Kěshì, wǒ xiàwǔ sì diǎn xiǎng qù yīyuàn kàn yīshēng. Nǐmen nà'er kěyǐ dǎ chūzū chē ma?

Xiao Wu: Ok. I will go over. But I need to go to the hospital to see a doctor at 4 in the afternoon. Can I take a taxi from there?

小喜：这儿有很多出租车。

Xiǎo Xǐ: Zhè'er yǒu hěnduō chūzū chē.

Xiao Xi: There are a lot of taxis here.

小五：好。我现在就去你的家。

Xiǎo Wǔ: Hǎo. Wǒ xiànzài jiù qù nǐ de jiā.

Xiao Wu: Ok. I will go to your house now.

小五到了小喜的家：

Xiǎo Wǔ dàole Xiǎo Xǐ de jiā:

Xiao Wu reached Xiao Xi’s house:

小五：你们在做什么呢？

Xiǎo Wǔ: Nǐmen zài zuò shénme ne?

Xiao Wu: What are you all doing?

小亮：我在泡茶给你们喝。

Xiǎo Liàng: Wǒ zài pào chá gěi nǐmen hē.

Xiao Liang: I am making you tea.

小喜：我在做中国菜给你们吃。

Xiǎo Xǐ: Wǒ zài zuò zhōngguó cài gěi nǐmen chī.

Xiao Xi: I am cooking Chinese food for you.

小五：太好了。我想喝茶也想吃中国菜。几时能喝到茶和吃到饭菜呢？

Xiǎo Wǔ: Tài hǎole. Wǒ xiǎng hē chá yě xiǎng chī zhōngguó cài. Jǐshí néng hē dào chá hé chī dào fàncài ne?

Xiao Wu: Great. I want to drink tea and want to eat Chinese food. When can I drink tea and have the food?

小亮：我的茶快要好了。你坐一下吧。

Xiǎo Liàng: Wǒ de chá kuàiyào hǎole. Nǐ zuò yīxià ba.

Xiao Liang: My tea is going to be ready soon. Please have a seat first.

小喜：我的菜也快要做好了。

Xiǎo Xǐ: Wǒ de cài yě kuàiyào zuò hǎole.

Xiao Xi: My food is almost ready.

小五：太好了。我一来就有茶喝，有菜吃了。

Xiǎo Wǔ: Tài hǎole. Wǒ yī lái jiù yǒu chá hē, yǒu cài chīle.

Xiao Wu: Great. I have tea to drink and have food to eat.

小喜：好吃吗？

Xiǎo Xǐ: Hào chī ma?

Xiao Xi: Is it delicious?

小五：很好吃啊。比我昨天在饭馆吃的好多了。

Xiǎo Wǔ: Hěn hào chī a. Bǐ wǒ zuótiān zài fànguǎn chī de hǎoduōle.

Xiao Wu: Very delicious. It's much better than what I ate at the restaurant yesterday.

小亮：茶好喝吗?

Xiǎo Liàng: Chá hǎo hē ma?

Xiao Liang: Is the tea good?

小五：很好喝。这是什么茶?

Xiǎo Wǔ: Hěn hǎo hē. Zhè shì shénme chá?

Xiao Wu: Very good . What kind of tea is this?

小亮：是中国茶。

Xiǎo Liàng: Shì zhōngguó chá.

Xiao Liang: It is Chinese tea.

小五：茶和菜都这么好，你们快点儿一起去开饭馆吧。我会天天去你们的饭馆喝茶，吃饭的。

Xiǎo Wǔ: Chá he cài dōu zhème hǎo, nǐmen kuài diǎn er yīqǐ qù kāi fànguǎn ba. Wǒ huì tiāntiān qù nǐmen de fànguǎn hē chá, chīfàn de.

Xiao Wu: Tea and food are so good, you should open a restaurant together. I will go to your restaurant every day to eat and have tea.

Statistics for Story [10]

554 Total Word Count

114 Number of Unique Words

68 (45.33 %) of the 150 HSK 1 words are used in this Story

84.84 % of the Story comprise of the Extended HSK 1 words

26 New Words

New Words	Pinyin	Explanation
就	jiù	At once, right away, as soon as, then, in that case
天天	tiān tiān	Everyday
如果	rú guǒ	If, in case, in the event that
过	guò	Over, cross, pass (time)
只	zhǐ	Only, merely, just, classifier for dogs, cats, birds and certain animals
要	yào	Want
到	dào	Arrive, up to

New Words	Pinyin	Explanation
		(verb complement denoting completion or result of an action)
快	kuài	Fast, quickly, soon
比	bǐ	Compare, contrast
为什么	wèishéme	Why
话	huà	Words
让	ràng	Let, allow
对	duì	To, towards
用	yòng	Use
可是	kěshì	But, however
走	zǒu	To walk, to go
还	hái	Also, still, yet
再	zài	Again
着	zhe	aspect particle indicating action in progress for e.g looking at (看着)
出	chū	Out
门	mén	Door
拒绝	jùjué	Rejected
已经	yǐjīng	Already, have
外面	wàimiàn	Outside

New Words	Pinyin	Explanation
看起来	kàn qǐlái	Looks like
课	kè	Class

[10] Daughter Wants to go to University
女儿要去大学

有一家人，爸爸，妈妈，儿子和女儿住在我家的前面。我天天上午去工作的时候都看见他们一家人一起出去。爸爸开车，妈妈坐前面，儿子和女儿就坐后面。

有一天，我走过他们家的时候，看见那女儿在车的外面，很不高兴，她不要上车。妈妈开着车门叫她上车，爸爸也叫她上车，可是她还是不上车。我听到他们一家人这么说：

女儿：为什么我不能去美国读书呢？我同学的爸爸妈妈都让他们去美国读书。我不要一个人在中国读书啊！

爸爸：你妈妈和我要去工作，你快点儿上车吧。

儿子：我也要上课啊。

女儿：我去学校也没用。你们不让我去美国读书，我现在读书读的这么好都没用。我不去学校了。我要在家里睡觉。不用读书了。

妈妈：女儿，你不能这样。我们回来的时候再说，好吗？已经上午八点了。很多人在看着我们。快点儿上车吧。

儿子：是啊。回来再说吧。如果我们还不走的话，老师会很不高兴的。

女儿就上了车。我还没看过她的爸爸开车开的这么快。我回到家的时候，看见他们在下车了。我听到他们一家人这么说：

女儿：爸爸妈妈一点儿都不爱我。你们只爱儿子，不爱女儿。

妈妈：你不要这样说吧。爸爸会很不高兴的。

女儿：我说的是对啊！你们不让我去美国读书，可是让儿子去。你们说，我不是一个好女儿吗？为什么儿子能去美国读书，女儿就不能去。

爸爸：我们现在不能不说了。是这样的。你妈妈和我只有钱让一个人去美国读书，不能让你们一起去。我们不是不让你去，只是我们有的钱太少了。

妈妈：女儿，你看你爸爸不高兴了。不要再说吧。我们快去里面，我还要做饭。

他们就走去里面了。后来，我就听不到他们在说什么了。我在想，为什么中国人就是这样，爱儿子的比爱女儿的多。我看过很多人都是这样的。

过几天，我再走过他们的家。今天，女儿看起来很高兴，我很想问她为什么这么高兴。她的爸爸妈妈看来还在里面。我就快点儿走过去问那个女儿。她对我说，美国大学已经拒绝了儿子。那儿子就不能去美国大学读书了。就这样，爸爸妈妈让女儿下个月去美国读书了。

Pinyin and Translation [10]

有一家人，爸爸，妈妈，儿子和女儿住在我家的前面。我天天上午去工作的时候都看见他们一家人一起出去。爸爸开车，妈妈坐前面，儿子和女儿就坐后面。

Yǒuyījiārén, bàba, māmā, érzi hé nǚ'ér zhù zài wǒjiā de qiánmiàn. Wǒ tiāntiān shàngwǔ qù gōngzuò de shíhòu dōu kànjiàn tāmen yī jiā rén yīqǐ chūqù. Bàba kāichē, māmā zuò qiánmiàn, érzi hé nǚ'ér jiùzuò hòumiàn.

There is a family, father, mother, son and daughter living in front of my house. Every morning when I go to work, I will see their family going out together. The father will be driving, the mother will sit in front, and the son and daughter will sit behind.

有一天，我走过他们家的时候，看见那女儿在车的外面，很不高兴，她不要上车。妈妈开着车门叫她上车，爸爸也叫她上车，可是她还是不上车。我听到他们一家人这么说：

Yǒu yītiān, wǒ zǒuguò tāmen jiā de shíhòu, kànjiàn nà nǚ'ér zài chē de wàimiàn, hěn bù gāoxìng, tā bùyào shàng chē. Māmā kāizhe chēmén jiào tā shàng chē, bàba yě jiào tā shàng chē, kěshì tā háishì bù shàng chē. Wǒ tīng dào tāmen yījiā rén zhème shuō:

One day, when I walked past their home, I saw their daughter outside of the car and looked very upset. She didn't want to get in the car. Her mother opened the door and told her to get in the car. Her Dad also told her to get in the car, but she still didn't want to get in the car. I heard their family say this:

女儿：为什么我不能去美国读书呢？我同学的爸爸妈妈都让他们去美国读书。我不要一个人在中国读书啊！

Nǚ'ér: Wèishéme wǒ bùnéng qù měiguó dúshū ne? Wǒ tóngxué de bàba māmā dōu ràng tāmen qù měiguó dúshū. Wǒ bùyào yīgè rén zài zhōngguó dúshū a!

Daughter: Why can't I go to the United States to study? My classmates' parents let them go to the United States to study. I don't want to study alone in China!

爸爸：你妈妈和我要去工作，你快点儿上车吧。

Bàba: Nǐ māmā hé wǒ yào qù gōngzuò, nǐ kuài diǎn er shàng chē ba.

Dad: Your Mom and I need to go to work, please get into the car.

儿子：我也要上课啊。

Érzi: Wǒ yě yào shàngkè a.

Son: I have to go to class too.

女儿：我去学校也没用。你们不让我去美国读书，我现在读书读的这么好都没用。我不去学校了。我要在家里睡觉。不用读书了。

Nǚ'ér: Wǒ qù xuéxiào yě méi yòng. Nǐmen bù ràng wǒ qù měiguó dúshū, wǒ xiànzài dúshū dú de zhème hǎo dōu méi yòng. Wǒ bù qù xuéxiàole. Wǒ yào zài jiālǐ shuìjiào. Bùyòng dúshūle.

Daughter: It is useless to go to school. You won't let me go to the United States to study. It is useless to study so well. I am not going to school. I want to sleep at home. No need to study.

妈妈：女儿，你不能这样。我们回来的时候再说，好吗？已经上午八点了。很多人在看着我们。快点儿上车吧。

Māmā: Nǚ'ér, nǐ bùnéng zhèyàng. Wǒmen huílái de shíhòu zàishuō, hǎo ma? Yǐjīng shàngwǔ bā diǎnle. Hěnduō rén zài kànzhe wǒmen. Kuài diǎn er shàng chē ba.

Mom: Daughter, you can't do this. Let's talk when we come back, ok? It's already eight in the morning. There are many people looking at us. Get in the car quickly.

儿子：是啊。回来再说吧。如果我们还不走的话，老师会很不高兴的。

Érzi: Shì a. Huílái zàishuō ba. Rúguǒ wǒmen hái bù zǒu dehuà, lǎoshī huì hěn bù gāoxìng de.

Son: Yes. Talk about it when we come back. If we don't leave now, the teacher will be very upset.

女儿就上了车。我还没看过她的爸爸开车开的这么快。我回到家的时候，看见他们在下车了。我听到他们一家人这么说：

Nǚ'ér jiù shàngle chē. Wǒ hái méi kànguò tā de bàba kāichē kāi de zhème kuài. Wǒ huí dàojiā de shíhòu, kànjiàn tāmen zàixià chēle. Wǒ tīng dào tāmen yījiā rén zhème shuō:

The daughter got in the car. I haven't seen her Dad drove so fast before. When I got home, I saw that they were getting off their car. I heard their family say this:

女儿：爸爸妈妈一点儿都不爱我。你们只爱儿子，不爱女儿。

Nǚ'ér: Bàba māmā yīdiǎn er dōu bù ài wǒ. Nǐmen zhǐ ài érzi, bù ài nǚ'ér.

Daughter: Mom and Dad don't love me at all. You only love your son, you don't love your daughter.

妈妈：你不要这样说吧。爸爸会很不高兴的。

Māmā: Nǐ bùyào zhèyàng shuō ba. Bàba huì hěn bù gāoxìng de.

Mom: Don't you say that. Dad will get very upset.

女儿：我说的是对啊！你们不让我去美国读书，可是让儿子去。你们说，我不是一个好女儿吗？为什么儿子能去美国读书，女儿就不能去。

Nǚ'ér: Wǒ shuō de shì duì a! Nǐmen bù ràng wǒ qù měiguó dúshū, kěshì ràng érzi qù. Nǐmen shuō, wǒ bùshì yīgè hǎo nǚ'ér ma? Wèishéme ér zǐ néng qù měiguó dúshū, nǚ'ér jiù bùnéng qù.

Daughter: I am right! You will not let me go to the United States to study, but you let the son go. Tell me, am I not a good daughter? Why can't I go to the United States to study?

爸爸：我们现在不能不说了。是这样的。你妈妈和我只有钱让一个人去美国读书，不能让你们一起去。我们不是不让你去，只是我们有的钱太少了。

Bàba: Wǒmen xiànzài bùnéng bù shuōle. Shì zhèyàng de. Nǐ māmā hé wǒ zhǐyǒu qián ràng yīgè rén qù měiguó dúshū, bùnéng ràng nǐmen yīqǐ qù. Wǒmen bùshì bù ràng nǐ qù, zhǐshì wǒmen yǒu de qián tài shǎole.

Dad: We will tell you now. It is because your mother and I only have money to let one person go to the United States to study, and we can't let the both of you go together. We can't let you go because we have too little money.

妈妈：女儿，你看你爸爸不高兴了。不要再说吧。我们快去里面，我还要做饭。

Māmā: Nǚ'ér, nǐ kàn nǐ bàba bù gāoxìngle. Bùyào zàishuō ba. Wǒmen kuài qù lǐmiàn, wǒ hái yào zuò fàn.

Mom: Daughter, you see your father is not happy. Don't talk about it anymore. Let's go inside, I still have to cook.

他们就走去里面了。后来，我就听不到他们在说什么了。我在想，为什么中国人就是这样，爱儿子的比爱女儿的多。我看过很多人都是这样的。

Tāmen jiù zǒu qù lǐmiànle. Hòulái, wǒ jiù tīng bù dào tāmen zài shuō shénmeliǎo. Wǒ zài xiǎng, wèishéme zhōngguó rén jiùshì zhèyàng, ài érzi de bǐ ài nǚ'ér de duō. Wǒ kànguò hěnduō rén dōu shì zhèyàng de.

They went inside. Later, I couldn't hear what they were saying. I thought to myself, why do Chinese love their sons more than their daughters. I have seen many people like this.

过几天，我再走过他们的家。今天，女儿看起来很高兴，我很想问她为什么这么高兴。她的爸爸妈妈看来还在里面。我就快点儿走过去问那个女儿。她对我说，美国大学已经拒绝了儿子。那儿子就不能去美国大学读书了。就这样，爸爸妈妈让女儿下个月去美国读书了。

Guò jǐ tiān, wǒ zài zǒuguò tāmen de jiā. Jīntiān, nǚ'ér kàn qǐlái hěn gāoxìng, wǒ hěn xiǎng wèn tā wèishéme zhème gāoxìng. Tā de bàba māmā kàn lái hái zài lǐmiàn. Wǒ jiù kuài diǎn er zǒu guòqù wèn nàgè nǚ'ér. Tā duì wǒ shuō, měiguó dàxué yǐjīng jù jué liǎo er zi. Nà er zi jiù bùnéng qù měiguó dàxué dúshūle. Jiù zhèyàng, bàba māmā ràng nǚ'ér xià gè yuè qù měiguó dúshūle.

After a few days, I walked past their home. The daughter looked very happy, I really want to ask why was she so happy. Her father and mother are still inside. I quickly went over and asked the daughter. She told me that American universities have rejected the son. The son can't go to an American university. So, Mom and Dad let her go to the United States to study next month.

APPENDIX A – HSK 1 VOCABULARY

Words	Pinyin	Explanation
爱	ài	to like, to love
八	bā	eight
爸爸	bà ba	father
杯子	bēi zi	cup, glass
北京	běi jīng	Beijing, capital of China
本	běn	a measure word for books
不	bú	no, not
不客气	bú kè qi	you are welcome, don't mention it
菜	cài	dish, cuisine
茶	chá	tea
吃	chī	to eat
出租车	chū zū chē	taxi, cab
打电话	dǎ diàn huà	to make a phone call
大	dà	big, old (age)
的	de	used after an attribute
点	diǎn	o'clock
电脑	diàn nǎo	computer
电视	diàn shì	television

Words	Pinyin	Explanation
电影	diàn yǐng	film, movie
东西	dōng xi	thing, stuff
都	dōu	both, all
读	dú	to read
对不起	duì bù qǐ	to be sorry
多	duō	indicating degree or extent
多少	duō shǎo	how many, how much
儿子	ér zi	son
二	èr	two
饭店/饭馆	fàn diàn / fàn guǎn	restaurant
飞机	fēi jī	plane
分钟	fēn zhōng	minute
高兴	gāo xìng	glad, happy
个	gè	a general measure word
工作	gōng zuò	to work, job
狗	gǒu	dog
汉语	hàn yǔ	Chinese (language)
好	hǎo	good, fine
号	hào	(for date and month) number

Words	Pinyin	Explanation
喝	hē	to drink
和	hé	and
很	hěn	very, quite
后面	hòu mian	back
回	huí	to come/go back, to return
会	huì	can, to be able to
几	jǐ	how many
家	jiā	family, home
叫	jiào	to call, to be called
今天	jīn tiān	today
九	jiǔ	nine
开	kāi	open, to drive
看	kàn	to look at, to watch, to read
看见	kàn jiàn	to see
块	kuài	a unit of money, same as *yuan*
来	lái	to come
老师	lǎo shī	teacher
了	le	used at the end or in the middle of a sentence to indicate a change or a new circumstance

Words	Pinyin	Explanation
冷	lěng	cold
里	lǐ	inner, inside, interior
六	liù	six
妈妈	mā mɑ	mother
吗	mɑ	used at the end of a question
买	mǎi	to buy, to purchase
猫	māo	cat, kitten
没关系	méi guān xi	tha's ok, it doesn't matter
没有	méi yǒu	there is not
米饭	mǐ fàn	cooked rice
名字	míng zi	name
明天	míng tiān	tomorrow
哪	nǎ	which
哪儿	nǎ ér	where
那	nà	that
呢	ne	used at the end of a question
能	néng	can, may
你	nǐ	you (singular)
年	nián	year
女儿	nǚ ér	daughter

Words	Pinyin	Explanation
朋友	péng you	friend
漂亮	piào liang	beautiful, pretty
苹果	píng guǒ	apple
七	qī	seven
前面	qián mian	front
钱	qián	money
请	qǐng	please
去	qù	to go
热	rè	hot
人	rén	human, person
认识	rèn shí	to meet, to know
三	sān	three
商店	shāng diàn	shop, store
上	shàng	up, above
上午	shàng wǔ	morning, before noon
少	shǎo	little, few
谁	shuí	who, whom
什么	shén me	what
十	shí	ten
时候	shí hou	time, moment
是	shì	to be, yes

Words	Pinyin	Explanation
书	shū	book
水	shuǐ	water
水果	shuí guǒ	fruit
睡觉	shuì jiào	to sleep
说	shuō	to speak, to say
四	sì	four
岁	suì	year (of age)
他	tā	he, him
她	tā	she, her
太	tài	too, excessively
天气	tiān qì	weather
听	tīng	to listen
同学	tóng xué	classmate
喂	wèi	hey, hello
我	wǒ	I, me
我们	wǒ men	we, us
五	wǔ	five
喜欢	xǐ huan	to like, to be fond of
下	xià	under, below
下午	xià wǔ	afternoon
下雨	xià yǔ	to rain

Words	Pinyin	Explanation
先生	xiān sheng	Mr., Sir
现在	xiàn zài	now
想	xiǎng	to want, would like
小	xiǎo	small, little
小姐	xiáo jiě	Miss, young lady
些	xiē	some, a few
写	xiě	to write
谢谢	xiè xiè	to thank
星期	xīng qī	week
学生	xué sheng	student
学习	xué xí	to study, to learn
学校	xué xiào	school
一	yī	one
一点儿	yì dián ér	a few, a little
衣服	yī fu	clothes
医生	yī sheng	doctor
医院	yī yuàn	hospital
椅子	yǐ zi	chair
有	yǒu	to have, there be
月	yuè	month
再见	zài jiàn	to see you again, goodbye

Words	Pinyin	Explanation
在	zài	to be in/on/at; in/on/at
怎么	zěn me	how
怎么样	zěn me yàng	how
这	zhè	this
中国	zhōng guó	China
中午	zhōng wǔ	noon
住	zhù	to live, to stay
桌子	zhuō zi	desk, table
字	zì	character, word
昨天	zuó tiān	yesterday
坐	zuò	to sit, to be seated
做	zuò	to make, to produce

Appendix B –HSK 1 Standard Course Book Vocabulary

Words	Pinyin	Explanation
啊	a	particle showing affirmation or defense
吧	ba	used at the end of an interrogative sentence to indicate guessing; used at the end of a sentence to indicate suggestion, decision or command; used after "好" indicating the tone of agreement or permission
给	gěi	give, to
好吃	hào chī	good to eat, delicious, tasty
口	kǒu	a measure word for members of family
您	nín	you (polite)
身体	shēn tǐ	body
问	wèn	to ask, to enquire
也	yě	also, too
一起	yīqǐ	together

Words	Pinyin	Explanation
不少	Bù shǎo	quite a lot, many, not a few
车	chē	car
吃饭	chī fàn	to eat a meal
大学	dà xué	university
分钟	fēn zhōng	minute
国	guó	country, nation
汉字	hàn zì	Chinese character
后	hòu	after, afterwards, later
回来	huí lái	to come back
今年	jīn nián	this year
没	méi	there is not
那儿	nà'er	there
你们	nǐ men	you (plural)
前	qián	before, earlier than
太。。。了	tài...le	too excessively
下面	xià miàn	under, below
学	xué	to study, to learn
雨	yǔ	rain
这儿	zhè'er	here
这些	zhè xiē	these

Words	Pinyin	Explanation
打车	dǎ chē	take a taxi
开车	kāi chē	drive, driving
里面	lǐ miàn	inside, interior
明年	míng nián	next year
朋友们	péng yǒu men	friends
前天	qián tiān	the day before yesterday
上面	shàng miàn	above
书店	shū diàn	bookstore
说话	shuō huà	speak, say, talk
他们	tā men	they,them (male)
她们	tā men	they,them (female)
听见	tīng jiàn	hear
学车	xué chē	learn driving
学生们	xué shēng men	students
有点儿	yǒu diǎn er	kind of
这么	zhè me	so, such, like this, this way
这样	zhè yàng	so, such, like this, this way
做饭	zuò fàn	cooking

Audio Files Download

You may download all the audio files at:

https://allmusing.net/blog/hsk-1-storybook-vol-3-audio-files/127/

The audio files are in 3 separate zip files. You will need to input the following **password** to download each zip file.

Pq95X?J7*M

If you encounter any issues when downloading the files, please do not hesitate to email us at feedback@allmusing.net

Made in United States
North Haven, CT
23 November 2022

27147106R00114